Grand Diplôme® Cooking Course

Volume 9

Grand Diplôme® Cooking Course

A Danbury Press Book

The Danbury Press

a division of Grolier Enterprises, Inc.

Robert B. Clarke   Publisher

This book has been adapted from the Grand Diplôme Cooking Course, originally published by Purnell Cookery, U.S.A.

Purnell Grand Diplôme Editorial Board

Rosemary Hume and Muriel Downes Principals, London Cordon Bleu Cookery School, England

Anne Willan	Editor
Eleanor Noderer	Associate Editor
Sheryl Julian	Assistant Editor
John Paton	Managing Editor
José Northey	Co-ordinating Editor
Peter Leather	Art Editor
Charles F. Turgeon	Wine Consultant
Joy Langridge	Consultant Editor

Library of Congress Catalog Card Number: 72-13896
© Phoebus Publishing Company/BPC Publishing Limited, 1971/1972/1979
Filmsetting by Petty and Sons Ltd., Leeds, England.
Printed in the United States of America

4567899

All recipes have been tested either at the Cordon Bleu Cookery School in London or in our U.S. test kitchens.

Note: all recipe quantities in this book serve 4 people unless otherwise stated.

Contents

From the Editor

A luxurious casserole of fillet of beef in a rich brown sauce, a guide to mixing the perfect cocktail, and blueprints for a gingerbread house are just part of the **Menus** in this Volume of the Grand Diplôme Cooking Course.

Let the skills of the London Cordon Bleu Cookery School help you welcome weekend guests to a superb cold supper of consommé with mushrooms, veal Parisienne and a delectable pear and chocolate gâteau belle Hélène. Bring the gathering to a close with a Sunday brunch of fragrant fruit coffeecakes, fresh from the oven. For a larger affair, enliven the cocktail hour with a roundup of assorted canapés or choose one of the **Pâtés and Terrines**, the spicy meat mixtures that can also double as a first course to a roast or steak.

Don't overlook the delicious yet simple dishes made from **Variety Meats**, such as deviled pig's feet and kidneys Turbigo, simmered with onions, sausages and mushrooms in a sherry sauce. You'll find another French favorite, **Crêpes** — thin lacy pancakes — are equally delicious whether stuffed with savory chicken or ham, baked with bananas and pineapple or served with a sweet sauce like orange cream, one of many in the second feature on **Sauces**. Compare the pleasures of our native American **Pancakes** with nockerln and pfannkuchen — fluffy versions from across the Atlantic.

The appeal of **Fruit Cakes** is equally traditional, from sugar-glazed upside-down apple cake to spicy fruit and nut-laden Christmas cakes, frosted with snowy-white icings, colored with roses, leaves and simple geometric patterns. Finally, celebrate the highlights of **Jewish Cooking** with festival favorites like Chanukah potato pancakes and the Hamantaschen triangular cakes baked for Purim. As the saying goes, you don't have to be Jewish to enjoy knishes (little stuffed pastry balls) and blintzes (fried pancakes), and challah, the famous Jewish bread. Bon Appétit!

Anne Willan

THE PASSOVER SEDER TABLE

A traditional platter is always placed on the Passover table beside the Haggadah, the book containing the story of Passover.

The platter contains parsley accompanied by salt water to symbolize the tears shed in bondage; a roasted egg representing the Passover festival offering; a horseradish sprout with some of the green tip representing bitterness; a lamb shank bone or chicken leg bone to symbolize the Pascal sacrifice of ancient days when each family brought its special offering; morar (horseradish sauce) to suggest the mortar used in building by the slaves in Egypt; and charoseth, made of apples, raisins, almonds, and cinna-mon moistened with wine — a morsel of sweetness to lighten unhappy memories.

Close to this platter is a white napkin interleaved with three sheets of matzo. Matzo is the unleavened bread that the women baked on their flight from Egypt when they had no time to let bread rise. During Passover, bread is not leavened and instead of flour made from grain, potato starch and matzo meal (from ground matzo) are used.

Two of the matzo between the white napkin are used in the ceremony and one, called the afikomen, is hidden. A reward is given to whoever finds it, then it is divided so everyone can eat a piece for good luck.

Gefilte fish balls, garnished with sliced carrots, shredded lettuce and parsley, are served with chrane (recipes are on page 13)

THE TRADITIONAL PASSOVER TABLE

This menu is typical of the dinners served on Seder night to celebrate the beginning of Passover. The symbolic foods are set on a platter on the table (see page 8) as part of the Passover service — these foods are always passed around the table for each person to taste. Passover is an occasion for celebration and large gatherings are not uncommon.

Traditionally a specially sweetened red wine is served at the Passover Seder. This is widely available here with a 'kosher for Passover' label. The wine plays an important part in the ceremony before the meal. Although only one variety is served, each glass is filled four times during the ceremony to represent God's four promises of redemption made to the children of Israel. At the conclusion of the meal, the host pours an extra glass of wine and opens the door to welcome the Prophet Elijah.

Chicken Soup with Matzo Balls
Hard-cooked Eggs with Salt Water
Gefilte Fish Balls with Chrane

Turkey or Chicken *Tzimmes*
with Passover Stuffing *Red Cabbage Salad*

Passover Sponge Cake *Passover Wine Cake*
Passover Macaroons
Compote of Dried Fruit

Kosher Red Wine for Passover

TIMETABLE

Morning
Make Passover sponge cake or wine cake. Make macaroons.

Hard-cook the eggs.

Make the chicken soup and store in refrigerator.

Make tzimmes and store in refrigerator.

Make stuffing for turkey or chicken but do not fill bird.

Make gefilte fish balls, poach them, and keep in refrigerator.

Make chrane and keep in covered container in refrigerator.

Make dried fruit compote and chill.

Make dressing for salad.

Make and cook matzo balls and drain.

Make salt water for eggs.

Cook carrots for gefilte fish balls garnish.

Cook lamb shank, make charoseth and roast egg for the traditional platter (see page 8).

Set table and assemble ingredients for final cooking from 4:30 p.m. for dinner around 8 p.m.

Order of Work
4:30
Assemble traditional platter and set on table with matzo. Set oven at moderate (350°F). Stuff and truss turkey or chicken.

4:45
Depending on size start roasting the turkey or chicken now or later. Baste the bird often; turn from time to time during cooking.

7:00
Complete and arrange the red cabbage salad.

7:30
Turn down oven to low (300°F) and put in tzimmes to reheat. Put gefilte fish balls in oven to reheat if serving hot.

8:00
When the ceremony is over, bring chicken soup to a boil and put the matzo balls, covered, in the oven to reheat.

If serving gefilte fish balls hot, put carrot garnish in oven to heat. Take out turkey or chicken and make gravy. Serve dinner.

You will find that **cooking times** given in the individual recipes for these dishes have sometimes been adapted in the timetable to help you when cooking and serving this menu as a party meal.

Jewish Cooking Consultants Doris and Leonard Julian have kept kosher for most of their lives. They had to abandon the dietary laws while living in remote places with the U.S. Army but even in Germany, Col. Julian managed to obtain kosher ingredients. Now, although they do not follow all dietary laws, they always observe all the holidays and take pride in welcoming the family to traditional feasts and in cooking the recipes handed down from generation to generation.

Hard-cooked Eggs
with Salt Water

Stir 1 tablespoon salt into 2 cups water until dissolved. Serve each person a peeled hard-cooked egg with a little salt water in a bowl for dipping.

Chicken Soup with Matzo Balls

2 quarts chicken soup (see page 20)

For matzo balls
1 cup matzo meal
$\frac{1}{2}$ teaspoon salt
2 eggs, beaten to mix
$\frac{1}{2}$ cup water

Method
Put the matzo meal and salt in a bowl, make a well in the center and add the eggs and water. Stir to form a dough and let stand 5 minutes; if too soft to shape, add more matzo meal and if too dry, add a little more water.

Dampen the palms of your hands and shape the mixture into walnut-sized balls. Drop them into a large pan of boiling salted water, cover and simmer gently for 20 minutes. Drain the balls, set 2–3 in each soup bowl and pour the boiling chicken soup over them.

Gefilte Fish Balls

3 lb mixed whitefish, pike and
    carp or any other
    firm-fleshed fish
2 large onions
1 sheet of matzo
$\frac{1}{2}$ cup boiling water
salt and pepper
2 eggs, beaten to mix
2 stalks of celery, diced
1 large carrot, diced

For garnish
5—6 large carrots, cut in
    diagonal slices
chopped lettuce leaves
    (optional)
sprigs of parsley

Method
Cut the fish fillets from the
bone and remove the skin or
have the fish man do it for you
but ask for the fish bones and
skin.

Finely chop or grind the
flesh. Grate 1 onion and
finely chop the other; soak
the matzo in the boiling water,
drain and crumble it into a
bowl. Add the chopped fish,
grated onion and seasoning.
Stir in the beaten eggs until
mxied.

Wet the palms of your
hands and roll the mixture into
2 inch balls. Lay the fish bones
and skin, chopped onion,
celery and carrot in a shallow
flameproof casserole. Place
the fish balls on top and add
water to cover. Cover with the
lid and bring quickly to a boil,
remove the lid, turn down the
heat to very low and poach
the fish balls for $1\frac{1}{2}$—2 hours.
At the end of this time, the
liquid should have reduced by
half — if it reduces more, add
more water during cooking.

To prepare the garnish:
cook the carrots in boiling
salted water until tender and
drain them.

To serve hot: drain the fish
balls, pile them on a platter,
pour $\frac{1}{2}$ cup strained cooking
liquid over them. Arrange
the hot cooked carrots around
the edge. Serve with chrane
(horseradish sauce).

To serve cold: cool the fish
balls in the liquid, drain them
and reserve. Strain the cooking liquid and chill it until
jelled. Pile the gefilte fish
balls on a platter, surround
them with chilled cooked carrots and chopped lettuce, if
you like. Stir the jelled cooking
liquid to soften it slightly and
serve as a separate sauce or
as an additional garnish for
the gefilte fish. Garnish with
sprigs of parsley, and serve
chrane separately.

Chrane
(Morar — Horseradish Sauce)

For 2 cups: cook 1 unpeeled
washed medium beet in boiling water for 20 minutes.
Drain and reserve the liquid.

Peel and grate 1 lb horse-
radish root on a grater. Add $\frac{1}{4}$
cup cooking liquid or enough
to make the horseradish
deep red, and 2 tablespoons
distilled white vinegar. Or
using a blender, work pieces
of horseradish root together
with the cooking liquid and
vinegar. Stir in salt and
sugar to taste.

Chicken Fat

Many Jewish meat dishes
are made with rendered
chicken fat because butter
contravenes the dietary
law against mixing milk
and meat.

To render chicken fat:
in a saucepan cook 1 lb
uncooked chicken fat, cut
in pieces, over gentle
heat until almost melted.
Add 2 large onions,
coarsely chopped, and
continue to cook until the
onion is golden. Cool,
then strain into a con-
tainer.

Store in the refrigerator
for about 2 weeks or in
freezer for up to 6
months.

Uncooked chicken fat
is available from kosher
butchers but some butch-
ers and supermarkets
also sell rendered chicken
fat.

Quantities
All the dishes in this menu
on pages 10—17 are
kosher for Passover and
serve 8—10 people.

The recipes on pages
18—35 are for traditional
Jewish specialties and
they follow the dietary
laws if made with kosher
ingredients.

All kosher commer-
cial products on sale in
the stores are marked
with the sign Ⓤ.

◀ *For gefilte fish balls, roll the
mixture into balls with the
palms of your hands*

Turkey or Chicken with Passover Stuffing

For chicken: fill a 4–5 lb chicken with stuffing, truss and roast as described in Volume 1 (chicken basquaise), substituting chicken fat for the butter. With the tzimmes, this will give enough for 8–10 people.

For turkey: fill an 8–10 lb turkey with double quantity of the stuffing and roast as described in Volume 8, substituting chicken fat for the butter. With the tzimmes, this will give enough for 14–16 people.

Passover Stuffing

2 sheets of matzo
1 cup boiling water
$\frac{1}{4}$ cup rendered chicken fat
1 green pepper, cored, seeded and diced
1 stalk of celery, diced
1 onion, diced
2 eggs, beaten to mix
salt and pepper

Method

Break up the sheets of matzo, put them in a bowl and pour boiling water over; set aside.

Melt the chicken fat and sauté the green pepper, celery and onion over low heat until soft but not browned.

Drain the matzo. Stir in the vegetables, chicken fat and eggs; mix and season well.

Tzimmes

3 lb chuck roast or brisket of beef
1$\frac{1}{2}$ cups ($\frac{3}{4}$ lb) large prunes, pitted
2 tablespoons oil
2 onions, sliced
8–10 carrots, peeled and cut in chunks
4–6 sweet potatoes, peeled and quartered
6 tablespoons honey
juice of $\frac{1}{2}$ lemon
$\frac{1}{2}$ teaspoon cinnamon
salt and pepper

Method

Soak the prunes, if necessary, according to package directions and drain them.

In a large flameproof casserole heat the oil and cook the onion, stirring occasionally, until golden.

Trim any skin from the meat, then set it on top of the onions; put the carrots, sweet potatoes and prunes around the sides. Spoon the honey over the meat, sprinkle with lemon juice, cinnamon, salt and pepper and pour over enough water just to cover.

Cover the pot tightly, bring to a boil on top of the stove, then put in a low oven (300°F) for 3–4 hours or until the meat is very tender. Add a little more water during cooking, if necessary; at the end of cooking, the liquid should be well reduced and rich. Taste the gravy for seasoning before serving.

Red Cabbage Salad

1 medium head of red cabbage, finely shredded
1 large Bermuda or sweet onion, cut in thin slices

For dressing
$\frac{1}{2}$ cup olive oil
1 clove of garlic, crushed
juice of 2 lemons
salt
black pepper, freshly ground

Method

Push the onion slices into rings and combine in a bowl with the cabbage. Whisk the ingredients for the dressing together and season to taste.

Toss the dressing well with the cabbage and onion, add more salt and pepper if needed, cover and let stand 1–2 hours in the refrigerator before serving.

In Yiddish, the word **tzimmes** means to make a fuss over someone or something, or a lot of people being very loud. It is the sense of the word meaning a lot of things mixed together that gives its name to the recipe here and on page 25.

Pour water over the beef for tzimmes before cooking with the vegetables until the meat is very tender

Passover sponge cake – made with potato starch – is a traditional dessert

Passover Sponge Cake

¾ cup potato starch
7 eggs
1½ cups sugar
grated rind and juice of 1 lemon
pinch of salt
confectioners' sugar (for
   sprinkling)

10 inch tube pan

Method
Set oven at moderate (350°F).

Separate 6 eggs and put the yolks in a bowl with the remaining whole egg. Beat until mixed and gradually beat in the sugar, lemon rind and lemon juice. Continue beating for 12–15 minutes or until the mixture is thick and light and leaves a ribbon trail on itself when the beater is lifted.

Sift the potato starch with the salt and stir into the egg yolk mixture with a metal spoon, making sure the potato starch is thoroughly blended.

Beat the egg whites until they hold a stiff peak. Stir about one-quarter of them into the potato starch mixture to lighten it, then fold in the remaining egg whites as lightly as possible.

Pour the cake mixture into the ungreased cake pan and bake in heated oven for 55 minutes or until the cake springs back when lightly pressed with a fingertip.

Invert the pan over a wire rack to cool, making sure that the top of the cake does not touch the rack (use a bottle or funnel as a stand if the pan has no legs.

When cold, loosen the sides of the cake with a metal spatula and turn out. Sprinkle cake generously with confectioners' sugar before serving.

Passover Wine Cake

9 eggs, separated
¾ cup sugar
¾ teaspoon ground cinnamon
¾ cup sweet red Passover wine
¾ cup matzo cake meal
¾ cup (2 oz) ground walnuts
¼ teaspoon salt
confectioners' sugar (for
   sprinkling)

10 inch tube pan

Method
Set oven at moderately low (325°F).

In a bowl beat the egg yolks, gradually adding the sugar until the mixture is very thick and light. Add the cinnamon, then stir in the wine alternately with the matzo cake meal and the ground walnuts.

Beat the egg whites with the salt until they hold a stiff peak, stir about one-quarter into the wine mixture to lighten it, then fold in the remaining egg whites as lightly as possible. Pour the batter into the ungreased cake pan and bake in heated oven for 1 hour or until the cake springs back when lightly pressed with a fingertip.

Invert the pan over a wire rack to cool, making sure that the top of the cake does not touch the rack (use a bottle or funnel if the pan has no legs).

When cold, loosen the sides of the cake with a metal spatula and turn out. Sprinkle cake generously with confectioners' sugar before serving.

Passover Macaroons

3 egg whites
⅔ cup superfine (bar) sugar
1 cup whole blanched
   almonds, ground
6 tablespoons matzo meal,
   sifted

If you like, substitute 1 cup unsweetened shredded coconut for the ground almonds. Makes about 30 macaroons.

Method
Set oven at low (300°F) and line a baking sheet with silicone paper.

Beat the egg whites until they hold a stiff peak. Beat in 2 tablespoons of the sugar until the mixture is glossy, then fold in the remaining sugar with the ground almonds and the matzo meal. Drop small tablespoons of the mixture onto the lined baking sheet, leaving room between the mounds for the mixture to spread.

Bake in the heated oven for 20 minutes or until the macaroons are crisp and lightly browned. Cool until warm on the baking sheet, then peel off the paper.

Compote of Dried Fruits

3 cups (1 lb) mixed dried fruits
   (pears, apricots, peaches,
   apples)
¾ cup sugar
1½ cups water
3 inch stick of cinnamon
3–4 whole cloves
1 lemon, thinly sliced
1 cup whole blanched
   almonds

Method
Soak the dried fruits, if necessary, according to package directions and drain them.

In a large saucepan heat the sugar with the water until dissolved, bring to a boil and simmer 2 minutes. Add the soaked fruits, the spices tied in a piece of cheesecloth, and the lemon slices. Cover the pan and simmer 20 minutes or until the fruits are tender.

Discard the spice bag, add the almonds and chill before serving.

Serve chicken soup with kreplach triangles, knaidlach (back) or lockshen (recipes are on page 20)

JEWISH COOKING

The traditions of Jewish cooking are ancient, ruled by laws laid down thousands of years ago and following customs developed over the years that today are almost as rigid as the laws themselves.

The dishes served on the Sabbath and on holidays all follow a pattern so the chances are that Jews, no matter where they may be living, are all eating similar food on the same festival. Often these recipes symbolize the meaning of the festival. For example, dairy foods are served during Shevuoth to suggest the purity of the Ten Commandments and at the New Year the apples and honey in many desserts symbolize the sweetness hoped for in the coming year.

Jewish food varies from country to country because recipes must be based on available ingredients. Many recipes that are regarded as typically Jewish come from Central Europe — the home of so many Jews for centuries — and beets, cabbage, potatoes, and river fish like pike and carp play a prominent part. The Jewish cooking of North America is eclectic — an amalgam of the recipes brought by Jews from all over the world. Jewish cooking here has a reputation for hearty, homey dishes — soups, stews, dumplings and superb homemade breads and cakes.

Many of the dietary laws ruling these dishes were originally based on hygienic precautions sensible for a people living in a hot Middle Eastern land. This means, for instance, that shellfish is forbidden because it deteriorates rapidly in a hot climate and the meat of the pig is excluded because it can harbor trichinosis.

The most important dietary rules are:
1 Not to eat anything that 'dieth of itself or is torn whether it be fowl or beast.'
2 To eat only meat adequately inspected, killed in the traditional way and drained of blood.
3 To eat only meat of animals with a cloven hoof that chew the cud and are quadrupeds — such as sheep, deer, cattle. They must be properly slaughtered after inspection. Only the forequarters of such animals are acceptable for kosher use.
4 To exclude birds of prey.
5 To eat only fish with fins and scales.
6 Never to mix milk and meat.
7 To process meat by soaking in cold water, then salting and rewashing to remove blood.

Some of the rules are less obviously based on reason. For example, the rule about mixing milk and meat appears absurd to non-Jews. But to Jews these laws are not only a way of extending religious beliefs into everyday life, but they are also a perpetual link with the generations of Jews who ate the same dishes, followed the same laws and were inspired by the same beliefs.

Note: the recipes on pages 18–25 are popular Jewish dishes that are served all year, and servings are for 4 people.

Chicken Soup

4½–5 lb fowl, including giblets and feet
2 onions
2 carrots
2 stalks of celery, including leaves
1 turnip or parsnip (optional)
1 bay leaf
6 peppercorns
salt

Method
Remove the fat from the chicken and use for other dishes. Scrub the feet well, blanch them, then peel off the skin.

Put the chicken in a kettle with the giblets, except the liver, the feet and remaining ingredients. Cover with cold water, bring to a boil and skim.

Cover the pan and simmer 1½–2 hours or until the bird is tender. Lift it out and drain to serve as an entrée.

Strain the soup, taste for seasoning and serve with matzo balls (see page 12) or any of the following soup garnishes.

Garnishes for Chicken Soup

Lockshen (Noodles)

Bring 2 quarts water to a boil with 2 teaspoons salt and crumble in 4 oz fine egg vermicelli pasta. Bring back to a boil and simmer 5 minutes.

Drain the pasta, rinse under hot water to wash away starch and drain again. Place in a soup tureen or in individual bowls, pour boiling chicken soup over it.

Knaidlach

scant cup matzo meal
salt and pepper
1 tablespoon ground almonds
pinch of ground ginger
pinch of ground cinnamon
2 eggs, beaten to mix
4 tablespoons rendered chicken fat
¼–½ cup boiling water

Makes about 20 knaidlach.

Method
Put the matzo meal in a bowl with the seasoning, ground almonds and spices. Make a well in the center and add the eggs, chicken fat and stir well so the mixture forms large crumbs. Add enough boiling water to make a soft dough, cover and chill 2 hours.

Wet your hands and roll the mixture into walnut-sized balls. Drop the dumplings into boiling salted water, cover with a lid and simmer 18–20 minutes or until the balls are light and almost doubled in size.

Drain the dumplings well, place them in a soup tureen or in individual bowls and pour over the boiling chicken soup.

Kreplach

2 cups flour
salt
2 eggs, beaten to mix
1 tablespoon oil
2–3 tablespoons water

For filling
1 small onion, very finely chopped
1 tablespoon oil
1 cup (½ lb) ground cooked beef or chicken
pepper
pinch of ground mace
1 teaspoon chopped parsley
1 egg, beaten to mix

This filling is only one of many alternatives. Makes about 60 kreplach.

Method
Sift the flour with a pinch of salt onto a pastry board or into a bowl. Make a well in the center, add the eggs and oil. Working with the fingers of one hand, draw in the flour and work to a firm pliable dough, adding water as necessary.

Knead the dough on a lightly floured board for 5–6 minutes or until very smooth and elastic. Cover the dough with a cloth and chill it 15 minutes.

To make the filling: in a covered pan cook the onion in the oil until soft but not browned. Take from the heat and stir in the beef or chicken, salt and pepper, mace, parsley and enough beaten egg to bind the mixture.

Roll out the dough very thinly and cut into 2 inch squares. Place 1 teaspoon filling on each square, dampen the edges and fold over to form a triangle, pressing the edges together to seal them. Let stand to dry for 30 minutes.

Drop the kreplach into simmering salted water and poach 10–15 minutes or until they rise to the surface. Drain them, place in a soup tureen or in individual bowls and pour over the boiling soup.

Beet Bortsch

4 medium fresh beets
¼ cup sugar
6 tablespoons lemon juice
1 teaspoon salt

For garnish
2 large potatoes or 2 eggs
(for hot soup), or 1 cucumber
(for cold soup)
¼ cup sour cream

Bortsch comes from Eastern Europe. There are many versions – this is one of the simplest and it can be served hot or cold.

Method

Scrub the beets, taking care not to break the skin. Trim off the roots and tops, discarding the leaves, and put the beets and stems in a pan with water to cover. Bring to a boil, cover with lid and simmer gently for 20 minutes. Drain and reserve liquid.

Slip the skins off the beets and discard; coarsely shred the beets and finely chop the stems.

Put the beets and stems back in the cooking liquid, add sugar, lemon juice and salt and enough water to make 2 quarts of soup, bring to a boil and cook for 5 minutes.

To prepare the garnish if serving hot soup: peel, dice and cook the potatoes in boiling salted water for 5–8 minutes or until just tender; drain and add to the soup. Or beat the eggs to mix, stir in a little of the hot soup and stir this mixture gradually back into the remaining soup (it should be hot but not boiling). Reheat, stirring, until the soup thickens slightly.

To prepare the garnish if serving the soup cold: peel the cucumber, split in half lengthwise and scoop out and discard the seeds. Dice or thinly slice it and sprinkle with salt, cover and let stand 30 minutes to draw out the juices (dégorger), rinse away excess salt, drain well and add to the chilled soup just before serving.

Whether serving hot or cold, top each bowl with a spoonful of sour cream.

Potato Kugel

4 medium potatoes, peeled
1 onion
2 eggs, beaten to mix
1 tablespoon flour
2 tablespoons rendered
chicken fat
salt and pepper

Baking dish (1 quart capacity)

Method

Set oven at moderate (350°F) and grease the baking dish with chicken fat.

Grate the potatoes and onion on a fine grater or cut them in pieces and work a few at a time in a blender – the resulting mixture should be mushy.

Watchpoint: the potatoes discolor very quickly so the grating or blending must be done very fast.

Add the eggs, flour, chicken fat and seasoning to the grated mixture and mix well. Pour into the baking dish and bake in heated oven for 30 minutes or until browned. Cut in squares or wedges to serve. **Note:** the same mixture uncooked can be used to stuff a turkey or chicken if ½ cup breadcrumbs are substituted for the flour. Makes about 3½ cups stuffing.

Potato Balls

4–5 medium potatoes, peeled
1 small onion, finely chopped
2 tablespoons rendered
chicken fat
1 egg yolk
salt and pepper

For coating
1 egg, beaten to mix
½ cup matzo meal
oil (for frying)

Method

Cook the potatoes in boiling salted water for 15–20 minutes or until tender. Drain them and mash or work them through a sieve or ricer.

Cook the onion in the chicken fat, covered, over low heat until soft. Take from the heat and stir in the mashed potato with the egg yolk and seasoning. Cool slightly then roll the mixture into 1–1½ inch balls. Coat the balls with beaten egg and roll them in matzo meal.

Heat the oil to 375°F on a fat thermometer and fry the potato balls until golden brown, then drain them on paper towels.

Watchpoint: do not fry too many balls at once. If they touch each other, they do not brown evenly.

Chopped Liver

¼ lb (½ cup) chicken or
calf's liver
¼ lb baby beef or beef liver
1 large onion, sliced
4 tablespoons rendered
chicken fat
3 hard-cooked eggs
salt and pepper

To serve
few lettuce leaves
1 celery heart, cut in sticks

Method

Soak the celery sticks in ice water to make them crisp.

Sauté the onion in 1 tablespoon chicken fat until soft but not browned. Broil liver for 5 minutes on each side or until cooked through. Finely chop or grind the onion, liver and eggs.

Stir in enough chicken fat to bind the mixture. Add ½ teaspoon salt and a large pinch of pepper, or to taste, and mix well. Cool and serve chopped liver on lettuce leaves on individual plates. Serve celery sticks separately. **Note:** to keep chopped liver for up to 5 days, pack the mixture into a crock or bowl and pour a thin layer of melted chicken fat on top. Store in refrigerator.

Schav Bortsch
(Spinach Bortsch)

1 lb fresh spinach
1 quart water
1 onion, finely chopped
salt
½ cup vinegar or ¼ cup lemon
juice
½ cup dark brown sugar or
to taste

For garnish
¼ cup sour cream
4 small freshly boiled potatoes
or 2 hard-cooked eggs, sliced

This soup can also be made with sorrel, when available. Although bortsch is usually made from root vegetables with a large proportion of beets, not all bortschs contain beets.

Method

Wash the spinach thoroughly, trim the leaves and chop them coarsely. Put them into a large pan with the water, onion and salt to taste. Bring ▶

to a boil and simmer 10 minutes. Add the vinegar or lemon juice and sugar to taste, cook 2–3 minutes more, then remove from heat and chill before serving.

Garnish each bowl with a spoonful of sour cream and a hot boiled potato or sliced hard-cooked eggs.

Knishes
(Basic Dough)

2 cups flour
1 teaspoon baking powder
pinch of salt
2 eggs
½ cup oil
2 tablespoons water
oil (for brushing)
beaten egg (for glaze)

3–4 inch plain cookie cutter

Knishes are small pastry balls filled with a variety of sweet and savory mixtures. If using a sweet filling, add 2 tablespoons sugar when making the dough. Makes 12–14 knishes.

Method
Sift the flour, baking powder and salt onto a pastry board or marble slab. Make a well in the center and add the eggs, oil and water. Mix these together with the fingertips, gradually drawing in the flour with the whole hand to form a firm dough; work lightly until smooth and chill 15 minutes. Set oven at moderate (350°F).

Roll out the dough one-eighth inch thick, brush with oil and cut out in 3–4 inch rounds. Place a spoonful of filling in the center of each round and pinch the edges together to make a ball.

Place the balls, pinched edges down, on a baking sheet and brush with beaten egg. Bake in heated oven for 30–35 minutes or until the knishes are golden brown.

Serve savory knishes hot as an appetizer or with cocktails.

Fillings for Knishes

Chicken Liver

1 cup (½ lb) chicken livers
6 tablespoons rendered chicken fat
2 onions, finely chopped
4–5 mushrooms, finely chopped
slice of dry bread
salt and pepper

Method
Broil the livers until lightly browned. In a skillet melt 4 tablespoons chicken fat and fry the livers until well browned; take out and reserve.

Melt the remaining fat in the pan and fry the onion and mushrooms until soft. Work the onion and mushroom mixture with the livers and bread through the fine blade of the grinder and season well.

Beef

½ lb lean ground beef
6 tablespoons rendered chicken fat
2 onions, chopped
¼ teaspoon allspice
salt and pepper
2 eggs, beaten to mix

Method
In a frying pan melt the chicken fat and fry the onion until soft. Add the ground beef and cook, stirring, until the beef is well browned. Add the allspice and seasoning and cool. Stir in the beaten eggs.

Sauerkraut

2 cups fresh or canned sauerkraut
¼ cup oil
1 onion, chopped
1 tablespoon brown sugar
pepper

Method
If using fresh sauerkraut, soak it for 15 minutes first. Wash the sauerkraut and drain it well.

In a flameproof casserole heat the oil, add the onion and cook until soft. Mix in the sauerkraut with the sugar and a little pepper, cover and cook over low heat, stirring occasionally, for ¾–1 hour or until the sauerkraut is golden and very soft.

If the sauerkraut shows signs of sticking during cooking, add a little water.

Potato

3 medium potatoes, boiled, drained, peeled and mashed
1 large onion, chopped
¼ cup rendered chicken fat
2 eggs, beaten to mix
salt and pepper

Method
Fry the onion in the chicken fat until soft, beat into the mashed potatoes and cool. Stir in the eggs with plenty of seasoning.

Cheese

2 cups dry cottage or pot cheese
1 large egg
1 large onion, chopped
¼ cup butter
¼ cup dry white breadcrumbs
salt and pepper

Method
Beat the cheese with the egg until soft. Fry the onion in the butter until soft and stir into the cheese mixture with the breadcrumbs and plenty of salt and pepper.

Sweet Cheese

2 cups dry cottage or pot cheese
1 large egg
¼ cup sugar
pinch of salt
2 tablespoons dry white breadcrumbs
grated rind and juice of 1 lemon
¼ cup raisins, chopped (optional)
sour cream (for serving)

Add 2 tablespoons sugar when making the dough for a sweet filling.

Method
Beat the cheese with the egg until soft and work in the sugar, salt, dry breadcrumbs, lemon rind and juice and the raisins, if used.

Serve the cooked knishes with sour cream.

Note: the recipes on pages 18–25 are popular Jewish dishes that are served all year, and servings are for 4 people.

Blintzes

2 eggs
½ cup flour
¾ cup milk, or half milk and
    half water (mixed)
pinch of salt
1 tablespoon melted butter
¼ cup butter (for frying)

*6–7 inch heavy frying pan or
    skillet*

When making batter for a meat filling, substitute water for milk, omit the butter and fry the filled blintzes in kosher margarine or rendered chicken fat. Makes about 12 blintzes.

Method
Beat the eggs in a bowl with a fork until mixed, then stir in the flour and milk alternately, still using the fork. Add the salt and melted butter and beat until smooth.

    In the pan or skillet heat the butter and add 1–2 tablespoons batter, quickly tilting and turning the pan so the bottom is evenly coated. Cook over medium heat until the batter is just set on top and golden brown on the bottom. (Blintzes are cooked on one side only.)

    Turn out onto a cloth and continue frying the remaining blintzes in the butter in the same way, piling one on top of the other to keep warm.

    Browned side up, fill the blintzes with one of the following mixtures, and roll up, tucking in the ends. Heat remaining 2 tablespoons butter in a large skillet and fry the blintzes until browned on all sides.

Blintzes are filled with meat or cheese mixtures before frying

Fillings for Blintzes

Meat

1½ cups ground cooked beef,
    lamb, veal or chicken
1 medium onion, finely grated
2 egg yolks
salt and pepper

Method
Mix the meat with the onion and egg yolks and season well. Serve the fried meat-filled blintzes with soup, or as a main course with potato kugel (see page 21).

Cheese

2 cups cottage or farmers'
    cheese
1 egg
2 tablespoons sugar
pinch of salt
½ teaspoon ground cinnamon

Method
Beat the cheese with the remaining ingredients until soft.

    Serve the fried cheese-filled blintzes with sour cream and blueberries or strawberries, or with honey.

Quick Chopped Herring

1 jar (2 cups) herring fillets
    in wine sauce with onion
2 hard-cooked eggs
1 small apple, pared and
    cored
1 slice of light Jewish rye
    bread (without seeds)
2 tablespoons chopped parsley
    or 2–3 sprigs of fresh parsley
    (for garnish)
light Jewish rye bread (without
    seeds) or pumpernickel
    bread (for serving)

Method
Drain the fish fillets and reserve the liquid. Chop or grind the herring and onion, 1 hard-cooked egg, the apple and slice of bread. Mix well and if the mixture is dry, add a little of the reserved liquid. Pile the mixture in a bowl.

    Halve the remaining hard-cooked egg, scoop out the yolk and sieve it onto the herring mixture. Finely chop the egg white and sprinkle over the mixture.

    Scatter the chopped herring with chopped parsley or decorate with sprigs of parsley. Serve chilled with rye or pumpernickel bread.

Glazed Corned Beef

4–5 piece corned brisket
  of beef
8–10 cloves
$\frac{3}{4}$ cup dark brown sugar
$\frac{1}{4}$ teaspoon dry mustard
$\frac{1}{4}$ cup pineapple juice or sherry

Method

In a heavy flameproof casserole put the corned beef with water to cover, cover with the lid and simmer $3\frac{1}{2}-4\frac{1}{2}$ hours (55 minutes per lb) or until the beef is tender when pierced with a skewer. Cool in the water.

Watchpoint: if the beef is not cooled in the water it will lose flavor.

Set the oven at moderate (350°F).

Drain the beef, reserving the liquid. Score the beef fat in diamonds, insert a clove in each diamond and replace in the casserole. Combine the sugar, mustard, pineapple juice or sherry and 2 tablespoons cooking liquid and pour over beef.

Bake the meat in heated oven for 45 minutes, basting every 15 minutes. Serve hot or cold, carved in thin slices.

If hot, serve with potatoes mashed with chicken fat.

Ideal accompaniments when serving the beef cold are potato salad or cole slaw and pickles.

Sweet and Sour Cabbage Balls

1 small green cabbage
1 lb ground beef
$\frac{1}{4}$ cup uncooked rice
1 egg
1 onion, finely chopped
1 carrot, grated
salt and pepper
$\frac{1}{4}$ cup lemon juice or vinegar
1 cup tomato sauce
$\frac{1}{2}$ cup brown sugar

Method

To make the filling: mix the beef, rice, egg, onion, carrot and season well.

Immerse the cabbage in a large kettle of boiling water, cook 1 minute, lift out and peel off the outer leaves. When these become hard to remove, immerse the cabbage leaves in water again and repeat until you have 12–15 large cabbage leaves; use the remaining cabbage for another recipe.

Place a spoonful of meat mixture in the center of each leaf and roll into a ball, tucking in the ends. Pack the balls close together in a skillet or shallow flameproof casserole, pour over the lemon juice or vinegar and tomato sauce and sprinkle with the sugar.

Add enough water just to cover, cover with the lid and simmer for about 20 minutes, then lower the heat and cook very gently for 40 minutes longer. If you like, simmer the balls for a total of 40 minutes on top of the stove, then remove the lid and bake them in a moderate oven (350°F) for 20 minutes or until browned on top.

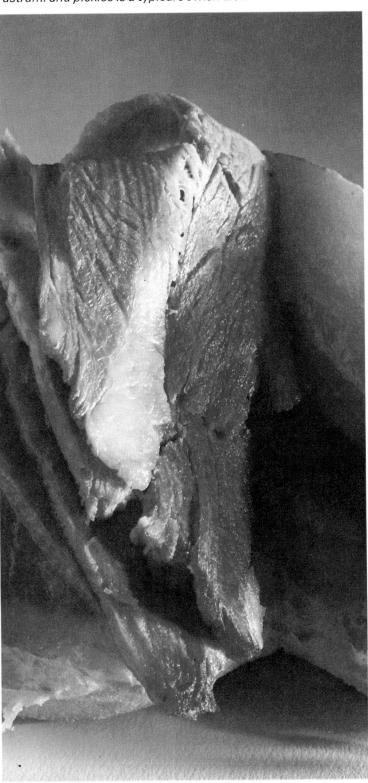

Pastrami and pickles is a typical Jewish dish

Beet and Cabbage Relish

1 lb beets, cooked and diced
½ small cabbage, shredded
3 stalks of celery, finely sliced
¾ cup wine vinegar or
    6 tablespoons lemon juice
3 tablespoons dark brown
    sugar
large pinch of salt
1 tablespoon prepared
    horseradish

Serve with cold meats.

Method
Heat vinegar or lemon juice and dark brown sugar in a saucepan until boiling, add the beets, cabbage, celery, salt and horseradish, cover and cook gently for 5 minutes. Chill.

Kichlach
(Drop Cookies)

1¼ cups flour
3 tablespoons superfine (bar)
    sugar
pinch of salt
3 eggs
⅓ cup melted butter
1 teaspoon vanilla

Makes about 4 dozen cookies.

Method
Lightly grease a baking sheet and set oven at moderately low (325°F).

Sift the flour, sugar and salt into a bowl and make a well in the center. Add the eggs, butter and vanilla and stir together lightly to a soft, smooth dough.

Place the dough in teaspoons (to leave room for the cookies to puff) on the prepared baking sheet and bake in heated oven for 20 minutes or until the kichlach are puffed and golden brown.

Dairy foods and **meat** are never served together in Jewish cooking. Under kosher law, they cannot even be cooked in the same pans, so a completely separate set of utensils must be kept for each type of cooking.

Meat can follow milk but dairy foods must not be served after meat, so desserts like **cheesecake** are always served at an all-dairy meal.

Recipes like **potato kugel** are made with chicken fat so they can be served at the same time as meat, but if the whole menu is a dairy meal, butter can be substituted for chicken fat.

Lockshen Kugel
(Noodle Pudding)

½ package (6 oz) medium-wide
    egg noodles
¼ cup butter
½ cup sour cream
1 cup (½ lb) creamed cottage
    cheese
¾ cup raisins
pinch of salt
1 egg, beaten to mix
1 cup milk
1½ teaspoons cinnamon
6 tablespoons sugar

Baking dish (1½–2 quart capacity)

Method
Set oven at moderate (350°F) and butter the baking dish.

Cook the noodles in boiling salted water for 8–10 minutes or until just tender; drain, rinse with hot water and drain again.

In a bowl toss the noodles with the butter until the butter melts, then stir in the sour cream, cottage cheese, raisins, salt, egg and milk. Mix the cinnamon with the sugar and add ¼ cup to the noodle mixture.

Pour the noodle mixture into the buttered baking dish, sprinkle the top with the reserved cinnamon and sugar and bake in heated oven for 30–35 minutes or until the pudding is set and brown.

Cut the noodle pudding into squares to serve hot or cold.

Prune and Farfel Tzimmes

½ lb prunes, washed and soaked
    in cold water to cover for
    30 minutes
1 cup farfel
3 cups boiling water
large pinch of salt
½ teaspoon ground cinnamon
grated rind and juice of 1 lemon
½ cup honey or dark brown
    sugar
½ cup butter

Farfel, or egg barley, is a pasta made from flour and eggs. It can be cooked and served alone as an accompaniment to meat dishes and poultry, instead of noodles, or combined with prunes, as in this recipe, to make a meatless accompaniment for a milk meal.

Method
In a saucepan combine the prunes with their soaking liquid, the farfel, boiling water, salt, cinnamon, lemon rind and juice, honey or brown sugar and butter. Bring to a boil, cover and simmer 30 minutes. Stir the prunes occasionally and if necessary, add a little more boiling water if the mixture looks dry.

Three-cornered Hamantaschen may be filled with poppyseeds or various other mixtures (recipe is on page 35)

JEWISH HOLIDAY COOKING

Almost every Jewish holiday has a special dish — whether it is fruit strudel to celebrate the harvest, Succoth; potato cakes or fritters fried in oil during Chanukah, the festival of lights; or the casserole cholent and braided challah traditionally served each week on the Sabbath.

On the following pages we also give a recipe for honey cake at New Year, Rosh Hashana; cheesecake for Shevuoth; and the famous three-cornered Hamantaschen eaten at Purim.

Cholent, a meat and barley casserole, and challah, the braided loaf, are traditionally served on the Sabbath

SABBATH

Cholent, a meat and vegetable casserole, and challah, a rich bread, often used to be served on the Sabbath, though today they are usually replaced by other, less traditional dishes.

In villages it was the custom for the housewives to deliver the cholent to the village baker to be cooked in his oven to eat on Saturday night; in this way the rule forbidding them to cook on the Sabbath (Saturday) was observed.

Two loaves of plaited challah are always served with the cholent to denote the collection of manna during the desert wanderings — enough manna for 2 days was always collected on the eve of the Sabbath.

Cholent

1½–2 lb piece brisket or chuck roast of beef
2 tablespoons rendered chicken fat, shortening or oil
2 large onions, sliced or diced
6–8 medium potatoes, peeled and halved or quartered
1 cup (½ lb) dried lima beans, soaked overnight and drained
½ cup pearl barley (optional)
2 tablespoons flour mixed with 1 teaspoon paprika, or to taste
salt and pepper
paprika (for sprinkling)

Method

In a Dutch oven or heavy flameproof casserole, heat the fat or oil, add the onion and cook until golden brown. Put the meat on top and add the potatoes, soaked beans and barley, if used, around the edge. Add boiling water to cover. Sprinkle the flour, salt and pepper on top and mix well.

Cover with the lid and simmer the meat mixture over very low heat for 3–4 hours or bake in a very low oven (275°F–300°F) for 8–12 hours or overnight. Sprinkle with paprika and serve with challah.

Challah

8 cups flour
1 tablespoon salt
2 packages dry or 2 cakes compressed yeast
2 cups lukewarm water
¼ cup shortening
1 tablespoon sugar
pinch of saffron, soaked for 30 minutes in ¼ cup boiling water (optional)
3 eggs
1 egg, beaten to mix (for glaze)

Makes 2 loaves.

Method

Sift the flour and salt into a large bowl and make a well in the center. Sprinkle or crumble the yeast over ½ cup of the lukewarm water and let stand 5 minutes or until dissolved. (If adding saffron liquid, use 1¾ instead of 2 cups water.)

Heat the remaining water with the shortening, sugar and the saffron liquid, if used, and stir until the shortening melts; cool to lukewarm.

Pour the yeast and shortening mixtures into the flour. Stir in enough flour to make a thick batter and sprinkle top generously with flour from sides. Cover bowl with a damp cloth and leave to rise in a warm place for 15–30 minutes or until bubbles break through the floured surface.

Add the eggs and work the mixture to a soft dough. Turn it onto a floured board; knead 7–10 minutes or until the dough is smooth and elastic, sprinkling the board with flour when necessary to prevent it from sticking.

Put the dough back into a clean and lightly greased warm bowl, turn it over and make a shallow crosscut on the top. Cover with the cloth and let rise for 1–1½ hours or until doubled in bulk.

Turn the dough onto a floured board and knead again for 7–8 minutes. Divide it in half and shape each half into a cylinder 12–14 inches long.

Cut each cylinder into 3 strips lengthwise, leaving them joined at one end and plait them; neatly tuck under the ends. For a plumper loaf, braid the bread with 4, instead of 3, strips. Transfer the loaves to a greased baking sheet.

Set oven at hot (400°F).

Cover the loaves with a cloth and let rise again in a warm place for 20–30 minutes or until almost doubled in bulk. Brush with beaten egg and bake in heated oven for 15 minutes. Lower heat to moderately hot (375°F) and bake 45 minutes longer or until the bread is brown and sounds hollow when tapped.

Honey cake and red wine are traditionally served at Rosh Hashana, the New Year

ROSH HASHANA (New Year)

The New Year is a time for optimism, and sweet cakes are baked in anticipation of a happy year. Honey is a favorite ingredient in these cakes and one traditional honey-soaked confection called tayglach can be shaped into knotted balls to indicate a year of continuity with no sudden breaks, or like a ladder in the hope that prayers will ascend to heaven.

Honey Cake

$\frac{2}{3}$ cup ($\frac{1}{2}$ lb) honey
$\frac{1}{2}$ cup strong black coffee
1 tablespoon brandy
2 eggs
$\frac{1}{2}$ cup dark brown sugar
2 tablespoons oil
1$\frac{3}{4}$ cups flour
3 teaspoons baking powder
1 teaspoon baking soda
$\frac{1}{2}$ teaspoon ground cinnamon
$\frac{1}{2}$ teaspoon ground ginger
$\frac{1}{2}$ teaspoon ground allspice
$\frac{1}{2}$ teaspoon ground nutmeg
$\frac{1}{4}$ cup whole blanched almonds, chopped
$\frac{1}{4}$ cup chopped candied peel
2 tablespoons raisins, chopped
2 tablespoons golden raisins, chopped
2 tablespoons chopped pitted dates

*2 medium loaf pans
(8$\frac{1}{2}$ X 4$\frac{1}{2}$ X 2$\frac{1}{2}$ inches each)*

Method
Set the oven at moderately low (325°F). Grease the pans and line them with a sheet of wax paper.

Mix the honey and coffee together in a small pan and bring to a boil. Take from the heat, add the brandy and let cool. In a large bowl beat the eggs until mixed, then beat in sugar and oil until well mixed.

Sift the flour with the baking powder, baking soda and spices and add the nuts and dried fruits. Stir this mixture into the egg batter alternately with the cooled honey mixture until the batter is smooth. Pour at once into the prepared pans and bake in heated oven for 30 minutes. Turn heat to low (300°F) and bake 40–45 minutes longer or until the cake springs back when lightly pressed with a fingertip.

Watchpoint: do not open the oven door until the cakes have been baking for at least an hour.

Turn the honey cakes out onto a wire rack to cool, then store in an airtight container for at least 2 days before serving.

Cookies or cakes made with a high proportion of **honey** always taste better after they have been left to mellow for several days.

Tayglach (Honey Balls)

2 cups flour
pinch of salt
$\frac{1}{2}$ teaspoon ground ginger or nutmeg
3 eggs

For syrup
1 cup honey
1 cup sugar
1 teaspoon ground ginger

Makes 24 honey balls.

Method
Sift the flour with the salt and spice. Beat the eggs in a bowl until mixed and stir in the flour to form a firm dough. Turn out onto a lightly floured board and knead until smooth. Divide the dough into walnut-sized pieces and roll each into cylinders about 4$\frac{1}{2}$–5 inches long; knot them, turning under the ends.

To make the syrup: in a shallow pan heat the honey with the sugar and ginger until dissolved, then bring to a rolling boil. Drop in 8–10 tayglach, reduce the heat and boil steadily for 7–8 minutes or until they rise to the surface.

Watchpoint: to prevent the syrup from boiling over, stand a wooden spoon in the pan but do not stir while the tayglach are cooking.

Lift the honey balls out with a slotted spoon, transfer them to a plate to cool and cook the remaining tayglach in the same way.

When cold, pack the tayglach in an airtight container between sheets of wax paper — they will keep for at least 2 weeks.

SUCCOTH

Succoth is a time of rejoicing — it commemorates the life of the Jews in the desert and also marks thanksgiving for the harvest. It is the custom to raise in the garden a booth (succah) — representing the desert tents — with 3 walls and a roof of branches through which the stars can shine at night. For the first 2 days of the festival, meals are eaten in the succah and dishes always include many harvest fruits and vegetables.

Apple Slice

2 cups flour
pinch of salt
6 tablespoons vegetable
   shortening
squeeze of lemon juice
8–10 tablespoons ice water
6 tablespoons butter

For filling
3 tart apples, pared, cored
   and sliced
3 tablespoons finely chopped
   candied peel
$\frac{1}{4}$ cup golden raisins
$\frac{1}{2}$ teaspoon ground cinnamon

To glaze
1 egg white or 1 egg, beaten
   to mix
$\frac{1}{4}$ cup whole blanched almonds,
   split in half lengthwise
granulated sugar (for
   sprinkling)

To finish
$\frac{1}{4}$ cup apricot jam glaze (see
   Volume 1)

Method

Sift the flour into a bowl with salt and rub in half the shortening with the fingertips. Mix the lemon juice with ice water and stir enough into the flour to make a dough that is soft but not sticky. Chill 15 minutes, then roll to an 18 X 6 inch rectangle.

Using half the butter, place small pieces of butter over two-thirds of the dough — at each end of the rectangle (leaving the center third plain) and fold in three to form a square (as for flaky pastry). Press the edges lightly with a rolling pin to seal; chill 15 minutes.

Give the dough a quarter turn and repeat the rolling and folding, first with the remaining shortening, then with the remaining butter, chilling between each rolling and folding. Roll and fold once more without fat; chill again.

Prepare the filling by mixing all the ingredients together.

Set oven at hot (425°F).

Roll the dough into a 10 X 14 inch rectangle and divide it into 2 long strips, one $4\frac{1}{2}$ inches wide, the other $5\frac{1}{2}$ inches wide. Transfer the smaller strip to a baking sheet and pile the filling down the center, leaving a 1 inch border of pastry. Brush the border with water.

Fold the second piece of dough in half lengthwise. Cut through the 2 layers (at the fold) at 1 inch intervals at right angles to the fold, cutting to within $\frac{1}{2}$ inch of the open edges. Lift the dough and place it over the filling so the cuts gape slightly, then seal the outer edges. Chill well.

Brush the top with beaten egg white or egg, scatter over the halved almonds and sprinkle with sugar.

Bake the apple slice in heated oven for 20 minutes, reduce heat to moderately hot (375°F) and bake 10–15 minutes longer or until the slice is brown and crisp. Transfer to wire rack to cool. Brush the slice with melted apricot jam glaze before serving.

For apple slice, pile the apple filling down the center of the smaller strip of dough

Place the second piece of dough over the apple filling. Seal the outer edges

Rolled Strudel

2 cups flour
1 tablespoon sugar
pinch of salt
1 egg
1 egg yolk
3 tablespoons oil
$\frac{1}{2}-\frac{3}{4}$ cup ice water
$\frac{1}{4}$ cup melted butter
   (for brushing)
confectioners' sugar
   (for sprinkling)

Method

Sift the flour, sugar and salt into a bowl. Make a well in the center, add the egg, egg yolk and oil and stir until mixed. Gradually stir in the flour, adding enough ice water to make a pliable but not sticky dough.

Knead the dough on a floured board for 2–3 minutes until very smooth and elastic, cover with a cloth and let stand 15 minutes to lose its elasticity.

Set oven at moderately hot (375°F).

Roll the dough as thinly as possible to a rectangle on a large pastry cloth, lightly sprinkled with flour.

Brush the dough with melted butter, spread the chosen filling evenly over the dough and roll up neatly by lifting the edges and gently pushing with the cloth.

Trim the ends of the roll and transfer to a greased baking sheet. Brush the top with melted butter and bake in heated oven for 35–40 minutes or until the strudel is crisp and brown.

Let the strudel cool slightly, then sprinkle it with confectioners' sugar if serving hot. If serving cold, sprinkle with sugar when cold.

Fillings for Strudel

Almond

Beat 4 egg yolks with $\frac{1}{2}$ cup sugar until light and thick. Stir in $1\frac{1}{2}$ cups whole blanched almonds, ground, and the grated rind of 1 lemon.

Cherry

Pit 2 lb Bing cherries or drain 2 cans cherries (1 lb each) and mix with $1\frac{1}{2}$ cups fresh white breadcrumbs or sponge cake crumbs, 1 teaspoon ground cinnamon, 1 cup sugar and 1 cup whole blanched almonds, ground.

Spread strudel with cherry filling and roll it up neatly before baking

SHEVUOTH

Dairy dishes are served during Shevuoth to symbolize the purity of the Ten Commandments given on Mount Sinai.

Strudel with cherry filling is cut into slices. The apple slice at back is topped with apricot jam glaze and blanched almonds

Cheesecake

For crust
2 cups graham cracker or zwieback crumbs
$\frac{1}{2}$ cup sugar
$1\frac{1}{2}$ teaspoons cinnamon
$\frac{1}{2}$ cup melted butter

For filling
2 cups (1 lb) creamed cottage cheese
1 package (8 oz) cream cheese
4 eggs
$\frac{1}{4}$ cup flour

1 cup light cream
1 cup sugar
pinch of salt
grated rind and juice of 1 lemon
1 tablespoon vanilla

8 inch springform pan

Method
Set oven at moderate (350°F) and grease the pan.

To make the crust: stir the crumbs, sugar, cinnamon and melted butter together until mixed and press evenly on the base and sides of the prepared pan, reserving $\frac{1}{2}$ cup for topping.

To make the filling: work the cottage cheese through a sieve. Beat the cream cheese until soft and beat in the sieved cottage cheese. Add the eggs one by one, beating well after each addition. Beat in the flour, then stir in the cream, sugar, salt, lemon rind and juice and vanilla.

Pour the filling into the pan and sprinkle the reserved crumb mixture on top, working it through a coarse strainer.

Bake the cheesecake in heated oven for 1 hour or until a skewer inserted in the center comes out clean.

Turn off the oven and leave the cheesecake inside for another hour; this prevents the cake from falling in the middle. Let it get quite cold, then remove the sides of the pan. Serve the cake on the pan base.

CHANUKAH

Chanukah, the festival of lights, is a favorite Jewish holiday though it is not a particularly important religious one. It celebrates the time when the perpetual light in the temple miraculously remained burning for 8 days with a single jar of holy oil. Today every household has a branched candelabrum that holds 8 colored Chanukah candles. Each night of the festival one more candle is lit so that on the eighth day, the whole candelabrum is brightly glowing. During the half hour that the candles burn, often traditional games are played. Chanukah is the time to serve fritters and potato latkes, both fried to signify the holy oil.

Potato Latkes
(Potato Pancakes)

6 medium potatoes, peeled
1 onion, peeled
½ cup flour
salt and pepper
2 eggs, beaten to mix
6—8 tablespoons oil or butter
   (for frying)

Makes twelve 3 inch pancakes.

Method
Grate the onion coarsely and put it in a bowl. Grate the potatoes onto a piece of cheesecloth, squeeze to remove any liquid and add to the onion. Stir in the flour, seasoning to taste and add the eggs.
Watchpoint: grate the potatoes quickly and fry the mixture at once so the potatoes do not discolor.

In a large skillet or frying pan heat 3–4 tablespoons oil or butter and drop in large spoonsful of the potato mixture to make 3 inch pancakes. Fry them until golden on both sides, take out and drain on paper towels. Heat the remaining oil or butter and fry the rest of the potato mixture in the same way.

Fritters

1 cup flour
pinch of salt
1 egg
2 teaspoons water
1 tablespoon oil
oil (for frying)

To serve
¼ cup sugar
1 teaspoon ground cinnamon

Makes 12—14 fritters.

Method
Sift the flour with the salt onto a board or marble slab. Make a well in the center and add the egg, water and the tablespoon of oil. Work together with one hand to a soft dough and knead lightly until smooth.

Divide the dough into walnut-sized balls, cover and chill 15 minutes. Roll out into the thinnest possible rounds.

In a frying pan or skillet heat a ½ inch layer of oil and fry the fritters one by one until they are light and puffy and golden brown on both sides, turning them once. Drain fritters well on paper towels and before serving sprinkle them with the sugar, mixed with the cinnamon.

Fritters are sprinkled with ▶ cinnamon and sugar for Chanukah, the festival of lights

PURIM

Haman, minister to King Ahasuerus of Persia, was determined to exterminate the Jews, but the King married a Jewess, Esther, and Haman's plans were foiled. The three-cornered pastries called Hamantaschen are always served during Purim. They symbolize Haman's three-cornered hat, that stood for his high office.

Hamantaschen (literally 'Haman's pockets') are so named because Haman hated the Jews so much that he was prepared to pay out of his own pocket (tasch) for their annihilation.

Hamantaschen

2 cups flour
¾ cup milk
2 tablespoons butter
1 package dry or 1 cake compressed yeast
pinch of salt
1 egg, beaten to mix
2 tablespoons sugar
¼ cup melted butter (for brushing)
chosen filling (see right)
2 tablespoons melted honey or 1 egg, beaten to mix (for brushing)

4 inch plain cookie cutter

For smaller pastries, use a 3 inch cookie cutter. Makes about 16 Hamantaschen.

Method

Heat the milk with the butter until the butter is melted, then cool to lukewarm. Sprinkle or crumble the yeast on top and let stand 5 minutes or until dissolved.

Sift the flour and salt into a warm bowl. Make a well in the center, pour in the yeast mixture, add the egg and sugar and mix to a soft dough. Turn the dough out onto a floured board and knead thoroughly for 8–10 minutes until the dough is smooth and elastic.

Place the dough in a lightly greased bowl, cover with a damp cloth and let rise in a warm place for 1–1½ hours or until doubled in bulk. Knead the dough lightly to knock out air and replace in the bowl, cover and let rise again in a warm place until doubled in bulk.

Set the oven at moderate (350°F).

Work the dough lightly to knock out the air and roll out on a floured board to ¼ inch thickness. Cut out 4 inch (or 3 inch) rounds with a cutter and brush each round with melted butter. Place a spoonful of the chosen filling in the center of each round, pull in the edges to form a tricorne. Pinch the corners, letting some of the filling show.

Set the tricornes on a greased baking sheet and let rise in a warm place for 15 minutes or until almost doubled in bulk. Brush the Hamantaschen with melted honey or beaten egg and bake in heated oven for 20 minutes or until golden brown.

Fillings for Hamantaschen

Poppyseed Filling

Warm 1 tablespoon honey with 1 tablespoon butter until melted and stir in 1 teaspoon lemon juice, ¼ cup whole blanched almonds, ground, and 1 cup poppyseeds.

Dried Fruit

In the top of a double boiler combine ½ cup raisins, ½ cup chopped pitted prunes, ½ cup chopped dried apricots, ½ cup fresh white breadcrumbs or cake crumbs and ¼ cup honey. Heat, stirring, over boiling water until the honey melts; cool the mixture. If too thick, add a little more honey from the jar; if too thin, add more crumbs.

Provide (Plum Jam)

Beat together until well mixed 1½ cups plum jam, grated rind and juice of 1 lemon, ½ cup whole blanched almonds, chopped, and ½ cup fresh white breadcrumbs or cake crumbs.

◀*For Hamantaschen, fold circles of dough into tricorne shapes, pinch the corners, letting poppyseed filling show*

Pickled onions and gherkins are an excellent accompaniment to liver pâté (recipes are on page 40)

HOW TO MAKE PATES AND TERRINES

Pâtés are savory mixtures usually made from chicken, calves' or pigs' liver with the addition of other meat, poultry or game. They can be smooth and velvety or coarse in texture and are often served as an hors d'œuvre with cocktails or as an appetizer. Smooth pâtés are served from the dish with a knife or spoon and spread on toast or crackers. More solid mixtures are cut in slices to serve on crackers or they may be eaten with a knife and fork with butter and warm toast served separately.

Substantial pâtés are generally served as a main dish with a salad accompaniment or as a buffet dish. This type is often called a terrine after the glazed earthenware casserole in which it is cooked. A terrine can have sliced meat or ham layered with the main mixture and all pâtés of this type are lightly pressed after cooking to make them easier to slice.

The meats for both pâtés and terrines should be well seasoned and contain some fat. A little brandy or sherry adds flavor and helps the mixture to keep well.

Pâtés and terrines keep well and improve in flavor if they are made 2–3 days before serving but they must be sealed with a layer of butter or fat (some mixtures form a thin layer of fat on top during cooking). Pâtés can then be kept in the refrigerator 2–3 days and terrines up to 5 days.

Points to remember

1 Simple terrines and pâtés are often cooked in a loaf pan or soufflé dish, but more sophisticated mixtures should be made in a covered casserole or terrine mold and the lid sealed with 'luting paste' so no flavor is lost (see box on page 42).

2 The terrine or casserole in which a firm pâté is to be cooked should be filled to the brim with mixture, then sealed with luting paste. The casserole or terrine is put in a roasting pan half filled with water and baked in the water bath in the oven according to the recipe.

3 To test if a sealed terrine is done, insert a thin skewer or larding needle through the hole in the terrine lid into the center of the mixture for 1 minute. If the skewer is very hot to the touch when withdrawn, the terrine is cooked. This avoids breaking the luting paste seal and no juice or flavor is lost.

4 If the lid has no hole, you must break the seal and lift the lid. Press the mixture and, if firm to the touch, it is done. If not, re-seal and cook another 10–15 minutes.

5 Soft pâtés (that do not need sealing) are served in the dish in which they were cooked or put after cooking, but firm mixtures are often turned out of the terrine or baking dish so they can be sliced more easily and neatly.

6 Pâtés and terrines should be served cold but not chilled, so take them from the refrigerator an hour or so before serving.

To clarify butter: cut regular butter into medium-sized pieces and melt it in a thick saucepan over low heat. Continue to cook until foaming well, pour the butter into a bowl and leave to settle.

Skim any foam from the top and chill; the clarified butter forms a solid cake on top. Discard any liquid beneath. If not to be used at once, melt the clarified butter down, pour it into a covered container and store in the refrigerator.

A ramekin is a small individual soufflé dish with straight sides. It is made of heatproof porcelain or earthenware, and may be plain or colored or decorated with flowers or fruits.

PATES FOR AN APPETIZER

Chicken Liver Pâté

1 cup chicken livers
½ cup butter
1 small onion, finely chopped
1 clove of garlic, finely chopped
salt and pepper
1 tablespoon brandy
pinch of thyme
¼ cup clarified butter

4 individual ramekins or dishes or a china dish (3 cup capacity)

This pâté is cooked on top of the stove.

Method
Remove any veins from the liver. In a pan melt half the butter and cook the onion and garlic until soft. Add the livers, increase the heat and sauté briskly for 2–3 minutes until they are firm to the touch.

Cool the mixture and chop finely, then work through a sieve; alternatively, purée it in a blender. Cream the remaining butter and beat into the liver mixture. Season well and add brandy and thyme.

Spoon the mixture into the ramekins or dishes, smooth the top and, if not serving at once, cover with a little clarified butter.

Rillettes

½ lb pork fat
1½ lb pork shoulder
1 duck, cut in quarters (optional)
1 cup water
1 teaspoon allspice
pinch of ginger
salt and pepper

4 crocks (1–1½ cup capacity)

Rillettes are a type of pâté made by cooking pork, rabbit or poultry for a long time until the mixture is easy to pound to a paste. It should be smooth and creamy but with a few fibers of meat left to give, texture.

Method
Cut the pork fat and pork shoulder into 2 inch cubes and combine with the duck, if using, and water in a flameproof casserole with a tight-fitting lid. Simmer over very low heat or in a low oven (300°F) for 3 hours.

Remove the bones and skin from the duck, return the meat to the casserole and cook, uncovered, for 30 minutes longer or until all the water has evaporated and the meat is simmering in fat. Strain off the fat and reserve it.

Cool the meat a little, add the spices and pull the meat into shreds with 2 forks. Reserve 1 cup of the shredded meat and purée the rest of the mixture in a blender. Beat in the reserved shreds of meat and season the mixture to taste.

Pack rillette mixture into crocks and spoon a little of the reserved fat on top to seal the mixture. Rillettes keep for up to 6 weeks in the refrigerator if the seal remains intact.

Creamy, smooth rillettes are delicious eaten with hot toast

Liver Pâté 1

1½ lb pigs' or calves' liver
½ lb piece of bacon
2 anchovy fillets (soaked in a
    little milk to remove the salt)
2–3 tablespoons heavy cream
    (optional)

For béchamel sauce
2 tablespoons butter
1½ tablespoons flour
1¼ cups milk (infused with
    slice of onion, 6 pepper-
    corns, bay leaf, blade of
    mace)
salt
black pepper, freshly ground
pinch of ground mace or
    nutmeg

*Soufflé dish or shallow pan
    (1½ quart capacity)*

Pigs' liver is excellent for pâtés as it is rich and full of flavor. Calves' liver is more expensive and more delicate in taste.

Method

Remove any ducts from the liver and cut it in small pieces. Cut two-thirds of the bacon into small pieces and pass through the fine blade of a grinder with the liver. Alternatively, work the bacon and liver in a blender.

Drain the anchovies and pound them in a mortar and pestle until smooth.

Make béchamel sauce and, when cool, mix with the liver and bacon, cream (if used) and pounded anchovies. The liver mixture should be very smooth. If it is not, purée it in a blender or work through a sieve. Slice the remaining bacon and use it to line the bottom of the pan or soufflé dish.

Pour in the liver mixture, cover the pan or soufflé dish securely with brown paper and set in a water bath. Then bake in a moderate oven (350°F) for 1 hour or until the mixture is firm to the touch. Take from the water bath, cover with wax paper and cool to tepid. Put a plate or board and a weight (about 2 lb) on top. Chill overnight. Turn out and cut in slices for serving. If the pâté is to be kept, cover the top with clarified butter and store in the refrigerator.

Barding Fat

In France, lean cuts of meat for roasting or braising are often 'barded' by tying a thin sheet of unsalted pork fat around them to moisten the meat during cooking. This fat is also often used to line molds for pâtés and terrines.

Barding fat is available at specialty butchers or sliced fat bacon can be substituted.

Liver Pâté 2

1 lb pigs' liver
½ lb ground veal
½ lb ground ham fat
2 cups fresh white
    breadcrumbs
½ cup milk
1 onion, finely chopped
2 tablespoons butter
3 tablespoons brandy or
    sherry
½ teaspoon ground allspice
¼ teaspoon ground nutmeg
salt
black pepper, freshly ground
2 eggs, beaten to mix
barding fat (see box)

Large loaf pan (9 X 5 X 3 inches)

Method

Line the loaf pan with the barding fat, reserving a piece for the top of the pâté.

Remove any ducts from the liver, cut it in small pieces and work it through the fine blade of a grinder.

Soak the breadcrumbs in the milk. Fry the onion in the butter until it is soft but not browned.

Mix the liver, ground veal and ham fat, soaked bread-crumbs and onion with the brandy or sherry, spices and plenty of seasoning. Stir in the beaten eggs.

Spoon the mixture into the lined loaf pan and cover the top with a piece of barding fat. Set the pan in a water bath and bake in a moderate oven (350°F) for 1 hour or until the mixture is firm to the touch.

Take the pan from the water bath, cool the pâté to tepid and cover it with wax paper. Put a plate or board with a weight (about 2 lb) on top and chill overnight. If the pâté is to be kept, cover it with clarified butter, then with foil and store in the refrigerator.

To serve, unmold the pâté, then turn it upright so the browned top is uppermost.

Pâté de Campagne 1 (Country Pâté)

1 lb ground veal or pork
½ lb pigs' liver, ground
¼ lb pork fat, ground
1 shallot, finely chopped
5 slices of firm white bread,
    crusts removed
¼ cup port
3 eggs, beaten to mix
small pinch of allspice
1 teaspoon thyme or marjoram
pinch of salt
6–8 slices of bacon

Medium loaf pan (8½ X 4½ X 2½ inches)

Method

Combine the ground meat, liver, pork fat and shallot in a bowl. Soak the bread in port and add to the meat with the eggs, allspice, herbs and salt.

Purée the mixture, a little at a time, in a blender or beat together thoroughly.

Line the loaf pan with bacon slices, fill with the mixture and press down well. Smooth the top, cover securely with foil and bake in a water bath in a moderate oven (350°F) for 1–1¼ hours or until the pâté is firm to the touch.

Cool the pâté to tepid, cover with wax paper, press it in the pan with a board and a light weight (about 2 lb) on top and leave until cold. Turn out the pâté and cut in slices for serving or cover with clarified butter to keep.

Pâté de campagne 1 makes a tempting appetizer when served with hot buttered toast

Pâté de Campagne 2
(Country Pâté)

1 lb veal, ground
$\frac{1}{2}$ lb raw ham, ground
1 lb pork, ground
$\frac{1}{2}$ lb pigs' liver, ground
$\frac{1}{2}$ lb pork fat, ground
$\frac{1}{4}$ lb salt pork, very thinly sliced
2 cloves of garlic, crushed
large pinch of allspice
salt and pepper
$\frac{1}{4}$ cup brandy or sherry
1 bay leaf
luting paste (see box)

Terrine (2 quart capacity)

Method
Combine the ground veal, ham, pork, liver and pork fat in a bowl with garlic, allspice and salt and pepper. Moisten with brandy or sherry.

Line the bottom of the terrine with salt pork and spoon the pâté mixture on top. Press down well, smooth the top and lay the bay leaf on it. Put on the lid, seal the join with luting paste and place in a water bath. Bake in a moderate oven (350°F) for $1\frac{1}{2}$–$1\frac{3}{4}$ hours or until the pâté is done when tested with a skewer inserted through the hole in the center of the lid.

Cool the pâté to tepid, remove luting paste, lid and bay leaf; cover with wax paper and press the pâté with a board and weight (about 2 lb) on top. When cold replace the lid and store in the refrigerator. Cut in slices to serve.

Ham Pâté

$\frac{1}{2}$ lb raw ham, ground
$\frac{1}{2}$ lb cooked ham, cut in $\frac{1}{4}$ inch strips
1 lb pork, ground
1 lb pork fat, ground
2 cloves of garlic, crushed
$\frac{1}{4}$ teaspoon crushed juniper berries
$\frac{1}{4}$ cup brandy
salt and pepper
6 slices of bacon

Large loaf pan (9 X 5 X 3 inches)

Method
Combine the raw ham, pork, pork fat, garlic, juniper berries, brandy, a little salt and plenty of pepper. Spoon one-third of the pork mixture into the loaf pan, lay half the strips of cooked ham on top, add another third of pork mixture, a layer of remaining ham and end with the pork mixture.

Lay slices of bacon on top and cover the loaf pan securely with foil. Place it in a water bath and bake in a moderate oven (350°F) for $1\frac{1}{4}$–$1\frac{1}{2}$ hours or until the mixture is firm to the touch when pressed.

Remove the foil, cover pâté with wax paper, cool to tepid and put a plate or board and a weight (about 2 lb) on top; leave overnight. Turn out and cut pâté in slices for serving.

Terrine Molds
Traditional terrine molds are made of ovenproof china or earthenware and are usually oval in shape. The lid must fit well and should have a hole for steam to escape and to allow for testing.

Terrine molds come in many sizes (it is important that the mixture fill the terrine completely). China ones are often decorated. Some very attractive terrines are made in beige bisque with the lid in the shape of a duck, rabbit or other animal or bird, suggesting the contents of the mold.

Luting paste is a flour and water mixture used to seal terrines. To make it, stir 6–7 tablespoons water into 1 cup flour with a teaspoon or your forefinger to form a paste. Do not stir too much or the paste will become elastic and shrink during cooking. Spread with the fingers, pressing well into the gap between the terrine and the lid.

Note: for storing times for these pâtés or terrines, see page 38.

PATES FOR AN ENTREE

Simple Terrine

1 lb veal or pork, ground
$\frac{1}{2}$ lb sausage meat
$\frac{1}{2}$ lb pigs' or lambs' liver, ground
8–9 slices of bacon
1 small onion, finely chopped
2 hard-cooked eggs, chopped
1 tablespoon mixed herbs (parsley, thyme, marjoram)
1 cup fresh white breadcrumbs
pinch of ground mace
salt and pepper
1 bay leaf
luting paste (see box)

Terrine or casserole (2 quart capacity)

Method
Combine veal or pork, sausage meat, liver, onion, chopped eggs, herbs, fresh breadcrumbs, mace, salt and pepper and mix thoroughly.

Line the terrine or casserole with the bacon slices and fill with the liver mixture. Smooth top and lay the bay leaf on it, cover with the lid and seal the join with luting paste.

Place the terrine in a water bath and bake in a moderately low oven (325°F) for 1–$1\frac{1}{2}$ hours or until the terrine is done when tested with a skewer inserted through the lid.

Cool the terrine to tepid, remove the luting paste, lid and bay leaf, cover with wax paper and press with a board and weight (about 4 lb) on top until cold. Replace the lid and store in the refrigerator. Turn out and slice for serving.

An ideal pâté for an appetizer is chicken liver (recipe is on page 38); here it is served two ways

Cut the finished terrine maison in slices and serve with wholewheat bread and butter

Terrine Maison

½ lb raw game (rabbit, squab, venison), pork or raw ham
½ lb sliced bacon
3 tablespoons sherry or port (optional)
1 bay leaf
luting paste (see box, page 42)
¾ cup jellied stock or ¾ cup consommé and 1 teaspoon gelatin

For stuffing
½ lb pigs' liver, ground
1 lb veal, ground
¼ lb pork, ground
¼ lb pork fat, ground
1 small onion, finely chopped
1 teaspoon mixed herbs (thyme, savory, oregano)
salt and pepper

Terrine or casserole (1½ quart capacity)

Method
To make the stuffing: combine the liver, veal, pork, pork fat, onion, herbs and salt and pepper and mix thoroughly.

Line the terrine or casserole with the bacon slices.

Cut the game (or pork or ham) into strips, pour over the sherry or port and season.

Spread about one-third of the stuffing in the terrine or casserole, press down well and scatter over about half the game. Repeat these layers, ending with a layer of stuffing. Smooth the top and lay the bay leaf on it. Cover with the lid and seal the join with luting paste.

Cook the terrine in a water bath in a moderately low oven (325°F) for 1¼–1½ hours or until the terrine is done when tested with a skewer inserted through the lid.

Cool the terrine until tepid, remove the luting paste, lid and bay leaf, cover with wax paper and press with a board and a weight (about 4 lb) on

top.

When cold, scrape any fat from around the sides of the terrine and fill up with jellied stock, warmed until melted. (If using consommé, sprinkle the gelatin over the surface, let stand 5 minutes until spongy, then heat gently until the gelatin is dissolved.)

Chill the terrine until the stock or consommé is completely set before turning out.

For terrine maison, first line the terrine or ovenproof casserole with the bacon slices

After layering the stuffing and strips of game in the terrine or casserole, cover with lid and seal with luting paste

Chicken and Calves' Liver Pâté

½ cup chicken livers
½ lb sliced bacon
little brandy or sherry (for sprinkling)
black pepper, freshly ground
1 tablespoon butter
1 clove of garlic, crushed
1 teaspoon thyme, chopped
2 tablespoons chopped parsley
luting paste (see box, page 42)

For stuffing
2 lb calves' or lambs' liver
1 cup milk
½ lb pork fat, ground
½ lb lean pork, ground
2 shallots, finely chopped
¾ cup heavy cream
2 eggs, beaten to mix
3 tablespoons brandy or sherry
salt and black pepper

Terrine (2 quart capacity)

This rich pâté can also be served as an appetizer.

Method
To make the stuffing: remove any ducts from the liver and soak in the milk for 2 hours. Drain, rinse and dry it thoroughly. Cut the liver in pieces and pass through the fine blade of a grinder. Mix the liver with the ground pork fat, lean pork and the shallots. If possible work in a blender for a few seconds for additional smoothness. Stir in the cream, eggs, and brandy or sherry and season well.

Line the terrine with the slices of bacon. Sprinkle with a little brandy or sherry and grind over a little pepper.

Remove any veins from the chicken livers and slice them. Sauté the livers briskly in the butter for 2–3 minutes, add the garlic and herbs and mix well.

Put half the stuffing into the terrine and scatter the liver mixture on top. Add the remaining stuffing and cover with any remaining slices of bacon. Cover with the lid and seal the join with luting paste.

Place the terrine in a water bath and bake in a moderately low oven (325°F) for 1¼–1½ hours or until the pâté is done when tested with a skewer inserted through the lid.

Cool the pâté to tepid, remove the luting paste and lid, cover with wax paper and press with a board and a weight (about 2 lb) on top until cold. Replace the lid and let stand in the refrigerator for at least 12 hours before turning out and cutting in ¼ inch slices to serve. Serve with salads.

Note: for storing times for these pâtés or terrines, see on page 38.

Turkey and Ham Pâté

5 lb roasting chicken or 5 lb uncooked turkey legs and thighs
1 lb fat ham, ground
1 lb fat pork shoulder, ground
$\frac{1}{2}$ teaspoon ground allspice
$\frac{1}{4}$ teaspoon ground cloves
2 cloves of garlic, crushed
1 teaspoon mixed herbs – thyme, oregano
3 tablespoons brandy
salt
black pepper, freshly ground
2 eggs, beaten to mix
2 bay leaves
$\frac{1}{4}$ cup melted ham or bacon fat (to finish) – optional

Soufflé or baking dish (2 quart capacity)

Method
Cut the chicken or turkey meat from the bones, discarding the skin. Grind the meat, reserving the breast if using chicken.

In a bowl mix the ground chicken or turkey, ham, pork, garlic, herbs, spices, brandy and plenty of seasoning. Stir in the eggs. Spoon half the mixture into the dish and, if using chicken, add a layer of breast meat. Add the remaining ground mixture and smooth the top. Top with the bay leaves, cover tightly with foil and set the dish in a water bath. Bake in a moderate oven (350°F) for $1\frac{3}{4}$ hours or until the mixture is firm to the touch.

Let the pâté cool to tepid, put a plate or board and a weight (about 2 lb) on top and leave overnight. If the pâté is to be kept, run a thin layer of melted ham or bacon fat on top, cover and store in refrigerator. Serve pâté in the dish.

Terrine of Pork

1 lb pork tenderloins
$\frac{1}{2}$ lb sliced bacon

For stuffing
1 small onion, finely chopped
2 tablespoons butter
1 cup ($\frac{1}{4}$ lb) mushrooms, chopped
1 teaspoon mixed herbs (thyme, savory, oregano)
salt
black pepper, freshly ground
$\frac{1}{4}$ lb calves' or lambs' liver, ground
$\frac{1}{4}$ lb sausage meat
1 cup fresh white breadcrumbs
1 tablespoon brandy or 2 tablespoons sherry
about 12 pistachios, shelled, blanched and halved (optional)
luting paste (see box, page 42)

Rectangular terrine or loaf pan ($1\frac{1}{2}$ quart capacity)

Method
Split the pork tenderloins, then pound them to flatten the meat. Line the terrine or loaf pan with the bacon.

To make the stuffing: cook the onion in the butter until soft, add the mushrooms and cook, stirring, over high heat for 2–3 minutes or until all the moisture has evaporated. Add the herbs with salt and pepper to taste and turn out onto a plate to cool.

Combine the cooled mixture with the ground liver, sausage meat and breadcrumbs. Add the brandy or sherry, pistachios, if used, and season well.

Lay one-third of the stuffing in the bottom of the lined terrine or pan, cover with about half of the pork tenderloin, add another layer of stuffing and cover with the remaining tenderloin. Add the remaining stuffing and lay any remaining bacon slices on top. Put on the lid and seal the join with luting paste.

If using a loaf pan, cover with a double sheet of brown paper and with foil, pinched or tied on securely.

Set the terrine or loaf pan in a water bath and bake in a moderately low oven (325°F) for 1–$1\frac{1}{4}$ hours or until the terrine is done when tested with a skewer inserted through the lid.

Cool the terrine until tepid, remove the luting paste and lid, or the paper and foil, cover with wax paper and press with a board and a weight (3–4 lb) on top until cold. To serve, turn out the terrine and cut into $\frac{1}{4}$ inch slices.

Terrine of Game

1 lb venison, bear or any well-flavored game
$\frac{1}{4}$ lb salt pork
$\frac{1}{4}$ cup port or sherry
large pinch of ground allspice or mace
salt
black pepper, freshly ground
2 shallots, finely chopped
2 slices of tongue ($\frac{1}{4}$ inch thick)
1 bay leaf
luting paste (see box, page 42)
1 cup jellied stock (made from any game bones with 1–2 veal bones, or a pig's foot for a good jell)

For stuffing
$\frac{1}{2}$ lb pork, ground
$\frac{1}{2}$ lb sausage meat
2 teaspoons mixed herbs (thyme, oregano, savory)

Terrine or casserole ($1\frac{1}{2}$–2 quart capacity)

Method
Cut half the game and all the salt pork into strips, lay in a dish and pour over the sherry or port. Sprinkle with spice, salt and pepper and shallots, cover and marinate overnight in the refrigerator.

To make the stuffing: grind the remaining game and add to the ground pork and sausage meat with the herbs. Season well and add any liquid from marinating the game.

Cut the tongue into strips and add to the marinated game strips. Press one-third of the stuffing into the terrine or casserole and lay half the marinated meat and tongue mixture on top. Cover with half the remaining stuffing, add the rest of the meat and finally the remaining stuffing. Smooth the top, press a bay leaf in the center, add the lid and seal the join with luting paste.

Cook the terrine in a water bath in a moderately low oven (325°F) for $1\frac{1}{4}$–$1\frac{1}{2}$ hours or until the terrine is done when tested with a skewer inserted through the lid.

Cool the terrine to tepid, remove the luting paste, lid and bay leaf, cover with wax paper and press with a board and weight (about 4 lb) on top. Leave overnight in a cool place, then fill up the dish with stock. Leave to set thoroughly before turning out.

Note: for storing times for these pâtés or terrines, see page 38.

Turkey and ham pâté – the layer of melted fat helps to store the pâté

Pâté en Croûte

For pastry
3 cups flour
½ teaspoon salt
¾ cup softened butter
3 egg yolks
7–8 tablespoons cold water
1 egg, beaten with ½ teaspoon salt (for glaze)

For filling
½ inch thick slice (about ½ lb) of lean ham, cut in strips
½ inch thick (about ¾ lb) veal cutlet, cut in strips
1 lb calves' or pigs' liver
1 lb ground veal
¼ cup brandy
¼ cup sherry
2 tablespoons chopped parsley
3 shallots, finely chopped
2 cloves of garlic, crushed
½ teaspoon ground allspice
¼ teaspoon ground nutmeg
¼ teaspoon ground coriander
salt
black pepper, freshly ground
2 eggs, beaten to mix
½ cup heavy cream

9–10 inch oval raised pie mold

Method

To make the pastry dough: sift the flour with the salt onto a board or marble slab and make a well in the center. Add the butter and eggs and work with the fingertips until it is fairly smooth. With the whole hand, draw in the flour and mix to a dough that is soft but not sticky, adding the cold water a little at a time. Knead the dough with the heel of the hand until it is very smooth, cover tightly and chill 30 minutes.

To make the filling: pour the brandy and sherry over the strips of ham and veal, sprinkle with parsley, cover and let marinate.

Remove any ducts from the liver and cut it in small pieces. Work it through the fine blade of a grinder and mix with the ground veal, shallots, garlic, spices and plenty of seasoning. Stir in the beaten egg and cream.

Drain the marinade from the ham and veal strips and add this liquid to the ground mixture. Set the mold on a baking sheet.

On a floured board, roll three-quarters of the dough to an oval about 10 inches across. Sprinkle generously with flour and fold in half, crosswise, like a turnover.

To shape the dough to fit the mold: with the hands pull the ends of the folded edge inwards to make a pocket. Roll the folded dough away from the open sides, towards the bottom of the pocket, until the hollow is large enough to line the mold. This technique avoids having to pleat the pastry around the sides of the mold. Lift the dough into the mold and press it well into the pattern on the sides of the mold.

Fill half the liver mixture into the lined mold, lay the veal and ham strips on top and pour over any marinade remaining. Add the remaining liver mixture and flatten the top.

Roll the remaining dough to an oval slightly larger than the top of the mold, lift it onto the mold and pleat the edges slightly to allow for shrinkage. Trim the edges, press them together firmly and flute with finger and thumb or decorate with pastry tweezers. Brush dough with egg glaze.

Roll out the dough trimmings, cut them into diamonds or crescents and decorate the top of the raised pie. Brush with egg glaze and chill 15 minutes. Set oven at moderate (350°F).

Bake the raised pie in heated oven for 1¼–1½ hours or until it tests done when a skewer is inserted in the center. If the pastry gets very brown during cooking, cover the pie with foil. Let the pie cool to tepid in the mold, then remove the mold and transfer the pie to a wire rack to cool completely.

The pie is best eaten within a day, so the pastry is still crisp. Cut it in slices to serve.

Raised pie molds are made in 2 pieces, with a hinge and slotted pin, so the mold can be removed easily from the finished pie. As it has no base, the mold must be set on a baking sheet before it is lined with dough.

Raised pie molds come in several shapes — round, rectangular, oval and square — and many sizes. The sides are usually 2–3 inches high and decorated with an embossed pattern that is impressed on the dough during baking.

Bacon Pâté

1 lb sliced bacon
1 lb ground pork
1 small onion, finely chopped
2 cups fresh white breadcrumbs
2 hard-cooked eggs, chopped
pinch of ground mace
2 eggs, beaten to mix
salt and pepper

Large loaf pan (9 X 5 X 3 inches)

Method

Line the loaf pan with 4–5 slices of the bacon; reserve 6–8 slices and grind or finely chop the rest. Mix this with the pork, onion, breadcrumbs, hard-cooked eggs and mace. Stir in the beaten eggs to bind the mixture and season. When thoroughly mixed, press a layer into the loaf pan and smooth the top. Cover with 3–4 slices of reserved bacon, then press in another layer of the meat mixture. Cover with the remaining bacon and fill up with the meat mixture. Smooth the top and cover with foil.

Set the pan in a water bath and bake in a moderately low oven (325°F) for 1¼–1½ hours or until the pâté is firm and a skewer inserted in the center for 1 minute is hot to the touch when withdrawn. Take from the oven, top with a small plate and a light weight (about 2 lb) and cool.

To serve, turn out and cut into slices. This pâté will keep 1–2 days in the refrigerator.

Pâté en croûte is cooked in a raised pie mold so the pattern is embossed on the pastry

For an unusual appetizer, try pears and walnut salad served with cheese sablés (recipes are on page 52)

A CLASSIC ENTREE HAS A NEW TWIST

After an unusual appetizer of pears coated with a creamy dressing, there comes a chicken in wine with a difference: it is broiled instead of cooked in a casserole.

In preparing and serving the chicken entrée consider using a top quality Bardolino from a major producer — Bretani, Bolla or Folonari — of a fairly recent vintage. Bardolino is one of those engaging wines from Italy that here are too often restricted to accompanying spaghetti.

Italian wines are diverse and the best of them that come in conventional (not straw-covered) bottles have considerable charm and sophistication. It may be a little harder to find the best American equivalent, Barbera, of the northern Italian red wines. This excellent, full-bodied red hails from California's north coast around San Francisco.

Pear & Walnut Salad
with Cheese Sablés
or
Eggplant with Crab

Broiled Chicken
with Red Wine & Mushrooms
Château Potatoes
Celery Mornay

Rice Cream with Tangerines
or
Pineapple Anna
with Coconut Macaroons
Red wine — Bardolino (Italy)
or Barbera (California)

TIMETABLE

Day before
Make cheese sablés; store in airtight container.
Make dressing for pears but do not add cream.

Make strawberry or raspberry sherbet and freeze; make macaroons and store in airtight container.

Morning
Make rice cream, cover and refrigerate. *Or prepare pineapple slices for pineapple Anna and keep covered in refrigerator.*
Peel and shape potatoes; keep in cold water.
Wash lettuce for pears, dry and store in plastic bag in refrigerator.
Put chicken pieces in marinade, cover and refrigerate.
Bake eggplants, make filling, stuff them and leave ready for browning.
Cook the celery, coat with mornay sauce and keep, covered, in the refrigerator.

Assemble equipment for final cooking from 7:00 for dinner around 8 p.m.

You will find that **cooking times** given in the individual recipes for these dishes have sometimes been adapted in the timetable to help you when cooking and serving this menu as a party meal.

Order of Work

6:45
Turn out rice cream onto platter, decorate with tangerine sections but do not add the whipped cream. Cover and keep at room temperature.
Whip cream and add to dressing for pears.
If decorating rice cream with rosettes, whip cream, put into piping bag and chill until needed.

7:00
Heat broiler.
Pare pears, arrange with lettuce on plates, coat with dressing, sprinkle with walnuts, cover and chill. *Or arrange macaroons on a platter.*

7:15
Start to broil chicken.
Melt butter and cook château potatoes.

7:30
If not already using oven broiler, set oven at hot (425°F) ready to brown eggplants and celery.
Transfer chicken pieces to broiler pan and baste often.

7:45
Transfer chicken to platter, keep warm and make sauce.
Put celery in oven to heat and brown.
Put eggplants in oven to heat and brown.
Transfer potatoes to dish and keep warm.

8:00
Serve appetizer.
Decorate mold with rosettes of cream just before serving. *Or complete pineapple Anna.*

Pear and Walnut Salad

2 large ripe pears, preferably Comice or Bartlett

For dressing
1 large egg
2 tablespoons sugar
3 tablespoons tarragon vinegar
6 tablespoons heavy cream, whipped until it holds a soft shape

For garnish
½ cup coarsely chopped walnuts
1 head of Boston lettuce

Method
To make the dressing: in the top of a double boiler, beat the egg and sugar together until thoroughly mixed, then add the vinegar. Cook the mixture over simmering water, stirring until it thickens enough to coat the back of a spoon. Cover and cool. Fold in cream.

Pare the pears, halve them and scoop out the cores with a teaspoon. Wash and dry the lettuce, arrange the leaves on 4 individual plates and put the pears on top, rounded side up.

Spoon dressing over pears and sprinkle with walnuts. Serve with cheese sablés.

To prevent pears from browning once they are peeled, sprinkle the cut surface with lemon juice. Coat them at once with dressing or sugar syrup (or whatever the recipe calls for) and serve as soon as possible.

Cheese Sablés

¾ cup grated Parmesan or dry Cheddar cheese
¾ cup flour
6 tablespoons butter
salt and pepper

Method
Sift the flour into a bowl. Add the butter, cutting it in with a small spatula and, as soon as the pieces are well coated with flour, rub the mixture with your fingertips until it resembles fine breadcrumbs.

Add the grated Parmesan or dry Cheddar cheese and season to taste. Press the mixture together to make a dough. Sprinkle the surface of the dough lightly with flour, wrap the dough in wax paper and chill for at least 30 minutes.

Set the oven at moderately hot (375°F).

Roll out the dough into a fairly thin oblong with a floured rolling pin. The dough tends to stick, so ease it free from the board with a spatula, if necessary.

Cut the dough into strips about 2 inches wide, brush them with beaten egg and cut the strips into triangles. Place these sablés on a baking sheet lined with silicone paper or foil and bake them in heated oven for 12–15 minutes or until golden brown.

Watchpoint: remove the baking sheet from the oven immediately and lift off the paper with all the sablés on it. Cheese scorches easily and, if you remove them one by one, the last ones could become scorched from over-baking.

Serve the sablés cold.

Eggplant with Crab

2 medium eggplants
1 cup (½ lb) backfin crab meat
salt and pepper
4–6 tablespoons oil
2 medium onions, sliced
2 teaspoons paprika
1 tablespoon tomato paste
2 tomatoes, peeled, seeded
   and sliced
½ teaspoon oregano
pinch of cayenne or few drops
   of Tabasco
2 tablespoons grated
   Parmesan or Gruyère cheese
1–2 tablespoons melted butter

Method

Wipe the eggplants, trim the stems and cut them in half lengthwise. Score the cut surface with a knife, sprinkle with salt and let stand 30 minutes to draw out the juices (dégorger).

Set oven at moderate (350°F).

Rinse the eggplants to remove excess salt and dry them with paper towels.

In a skillet heat 2–3 tablespoons oil and fry the eggplants, cut side down, until brown. Take them out, set on a baking sheet and bake in heated oven for 10–15 minutes or until tender.

Cook the onions in the remaining oil until soft, stir in the paprika, cook over low heat for ½ minute and add the tomato paste, tomatoes, oregano and cayenne or Tabasco. Season and cook until the mixture is thick and pulpy.

Scoop out the flesh from the baked eggplants, reserv-ing the shells, add flesh to the tomato mixture and cook 2–3 minutes longer.

Flake the crab meat with a fork, add to the pan and heat thoroughly. Pile this mixture into the eggplant shells, sprinkle with cheese and melted butter and bake in a hot oven (425°F) for 6–7 minutes or until brown.

Eggplant halves are filled with onion, tomato, crab meat and cheese and baked until golden brown

Broiled chicken with red wine and mushrooms is garnished with fresh watercress

Entrée

Broiled Chicken with Red Wine and Mushrooms

6–8 chicken pieces (breasts or thighs)
1–2 tablespoons oil (for broiling)
¾ cup chicken stock
kneaded butter (made with 1 tablespoon butter and 1½ teaspoons flour), or 1 teaspoon arrowroot (mixed to a paste with 1 tablespoon water)
bunch of watercress (for garnish)

For marinade
1–2 cups (¼–½ lb) mushrooms, thickly sliced
3 tablespoons olive oil
2 shallots, finely chopped
1 cup red wine
bouquet garni
salt
black pepper, freshly ground

Method
To prepare the marinade: mix the oil, shallots, wine and bouquet garni with a little salt and pepper and pour over the mushrooms.

Lay the chicken pieces on a flat shallow dish (not metal) and pour over the marinade. Cover and leave at room temperature for 1–2 hours or up to 6 hours in the refrigerator.

If using an electric or gas broiler, turn it on, take the pieces of chicken from the marinade, brush them with a little oil and broil on a rack for 6 minutes on each side, allowing 1–2 minutes longer on the skin side so it browns well.

Slide the chicken pieces off the rack into the broiling pan, spoon over the marinade with the mushrooms, discarding the bouquet garni.

Replace the pan under the broiler and cook 10–15 minutes longer or until the chicken is very tender. Baste often with marinade and lower the pan after the first few minutes if the chicken pieces get very brown.

Arrange the chicken pieces on a hot platter, pour contents of the broiler pan into a saucepan, add the chicken stock and bring to a boil. Thicken slightly by whisking in the kneaded butter, a piece at a time, and simmering the sauce for 2 minutes, or add the arrowroot paste and bring just to a boil.

Season to taste, spoon the sauce over the chicken pieces and garnish the dish with watercress. Serve with château potatoes and celery mornay.

Note: if using a charcoal grill, cook the chicken pieces completely over the coals, brushing often with oil to prevent them from drying. Strain the marinade, reserving the mushrooms and discarding the bouquet garni, and boil until reduced by half. Add the stock, put back the mushrooms and make the sauce as above.

Spoon the marinade over the browned chicken pieces, then continue broiling until tender

Accompaniments to entrée

Château Potatoes

10–12 small new potatoes, or 3–4 medium potatoes
3–4 tablespoons butter
salt

Method
If using medium potatoes, peel them, cut in quarters lengthwise and trim off the sharp edges with a vegetable peeler. Blanch them by putting in cold water and bringing to a boil, then drain. If using new potatoes, scrub them with a pot scrubber or small brush to remove the skin, or use a vegetable peeler.

In a flameproof casserole melt the butter, add the potatoes and cook over moderate heat until golden brown all over, occasionally shaking to turn them and prevent them from sticking. Sprinkle lightly with salt, cover and bake in a hot oven (400°F) for 10–12 minutes or until tender.

Celery Mornay

1 bunch of celery
1–1½ cups chicken stock
salt and pepper
mornay sauce, made with 3 tablespoons butter, 3 tablespoons flour, 2 cups milk, ½ cup grated Gruyère cheese and 1 teaspoon prepared or Dijon-style mustard
¼ cup grated Gruyère cheese (for sprinkling)

Method
Wash the celery, trim the root and leaves and cut the stalks into 2-inch lengths. Put the celery into a pan with enough chicken stock to cover, add seasoning, cover and simmer 20 minutes or until the celery is tender; drain.

Transfer the celery to a shallow baking dish and spoon over mornay sauce to coat. Sprinkle with grated Gruyère cheese and bake in a hot oven (400°F) for 10–15 minutes or until browned; or brown celery under the broiler.

Sprinkle tangerine rind over the cream-covered rice cream and arrange tangerine sections around

Dessert

Rice Cream with Tangerines

3 tablespoons rice
4–5 tangerines
$2\frac{1}{2}$–3 cups milk
6 sugar cubes
1 envelope gelatin
$\frac{1}{4}$ cup granulated sugar
1 egg white (optional)
$\frac{3}{4}$ cup heavy cream, whipped
    until it holds a soft shape
$\frac{1}{2}$ cup heavy cream, stiffly
    whipped (for decoration) –
    optional

Fluted or ring mold (5 cup capacity); pastry bag and medium star tube (optional)

Method

Lightly oil the mold.

Rinse the rice in cold water, drain, put it in a pan with $2\frac{1}{2}$ cups of the milk and cook over very low heat for 30–35 minutes until the rice is very tender, stirring occasionally. If the mixture gets too thick, add more milk. When cooked, it should drop easily from a spoon. Keep warm.

Rub the sugar cubes over the rind of 2 of the tangerines until they are soaked with the zest (oil). Halve them, squeeze out the juice and strain it into a small pan. Sprinkle over the gelatin and let stand 5 minutes until spongy.

Dissolve the gelatin over a pan of hot water and stir it, with the sugar cubes, into the warm rice. Stir until the sugar has dissolved and stir in the $\frac{1}{4}$ cup granulated sugar. Leave the rice until cold.

Stiffly beat the egg white, if using, and fold into the lightly whipped cream. When the rice is cold and beginning to thicken, fold in the egg white

and cream mixture and pour into the prepared mold. Cover and chill 2 hours or until set.

Peel a little rind from the remaining tangerines with a vegetable peeler, cut into very fine strips and blanch them in boiling water for 5 minutes. Drain them, refresh and drain again. Peel the tangerines, separate the sections and snip the central edges, removing the seeds.

An hour or two before serving, turn out the rice cream onto a platter and sprinkle the tangerine rind on top. Arrange tangerine sections around the edge or fill the center with them if using a ring mold. Using a pastry bag fitted with a medium star tube, decorate the mold with rosettes of whipped cream, if you like.

Alternative dessert

Pineapple Anna

4 thick slices of fresh pineapple,
    core removed
1 large orange
1 pint strawberry or raspberry
    sherbet (see Volume 11)
about $\frac{1}{4}$ cup sugar (for
    sprinkling)
3 tablespoons kirsch

Method

Cut the rind and pith from orange with a serrated-edge knife, using a sawing motion. Cut orange, crosswise, into 4 thick slices, discarding end slices.

Put the pineapple and orange slices into a bowl, sprinkle them with sugar to taste and pour over the

kirsch. Cover and chill about 1 hour.

Just before serving, arrange the pineapple slices on 4 individual plates, put the orange slices symmetrically on top and finish with a scoop of sherbet. Pour over juice from the fruit and serve at once with coconut macaroons.

Coconut Macaroons

$1\frac{1}{2}$ cups shredded sweetened
    coconut
3 egg whites
$\frac{3}{4}$ cup sugar
1 teaspoon vanilla
few whole blanched almonds
    (for decoration)

Silicone paper

Makes 34–36 macaroons.

Coconut macaroons, decorated with blanched almonds, are ideal accompaniments to pineapple Anna

Method

Set the oven at moderately low (325°F) and line a baking sheet with the silicone paper.

Stiffly whip the egg whites, add $\frac{1}{4}$ cup sugar and continue beating until the mixture is glossy. Fold in the remaining sugar, then the coconut and vanilla.

Drop tablespoons of the mixture on the prepared baking sheet and top each one with a blanched almond. Bake in the heated oven for 20–25 minutes or until the macaroons are golden brown. Let cool slightly, then peel off the paper and transfer the macaroons to a wire rack to cool completely.

How to make fruit cakes

In the old days, fruit cakes were a way of enjoying fruit during the winter because the cakes could be made months ahead and then stored to be eaten in the cold weather. The flavor of fruit cakes improves with age. In fact, if well saturated with spirits and stored in an airtight container, a cake can be enjoyed as long as 25 years after baking.

Today, even though fresh fruit is available all year, these delicious cakes are still a wonderful treat as well as a useful standby for unexpected guests.

Points to remember

1 Candied and dried fruits add flavor and richness to a cake and also act as preservatives. Often nuts are added for a variation in texture as well as taste.

Most fruit cakes will become moister and their flavors will be enhanced if they are kept in an airtight container for 1–2 weeks.

2 Really rich fruit cakes, such as Christmas cakes, can be kept for a year or more and must be stored at least 4–6 weeks for their full richness to develop.

The flavor improves even more if from time to time during storage the cake is pierced in several places with a skewer, then sprinkled with a little sherry, brandy, rum or whiskey.

3 Candied and dried fruits for use in cakes should be moist and soft — if they seem at all dry and hard, soak them in hot water for a few minutes to soften them, but be sure to dry them thoroughly on paper towels before adding to the cake or else they will fall to the bottom of the cake.

When candied cherries are very moist and sticky, they too should be soaked in hot water to remove the syrupy coating, then dried thoroughly.

4 The greatest problem with fruit cakes is that the fruit tends to separate and fall to the bottom of the cake — this is particularly likely to happen when heavy fruit, like whole candied cherries, is added to a light cake batter. One way to help prevent this is to toss the fruit in flour so that it is thoroughly coated before it is added to the mixture.

Drafts produced by opening the oven door too soon can also cause fruit to fall to the bottom of the cake.

5 A fruit cake is done when a skewer or toothpick inserted in the center comes out clean — the cake will also shrink from the sides of the pan, but if the cake is rich in fruit, shrinkage will be slight. Fruit cakes are best cooled in the pan, then removed after about 30 minutes before they get quite cold.

The general rules given in our first feature on cake-making in Volume 1 also apply to fruit cakes.

Press the strip around sides of pan so folded cut edge overlaps base

Place the circle of paper in the base to hold the overlap in place

Lining Cake Pans for Fruit Cakes

For a round cake pan: brush the sides and base of a springform pan with melted shortening. Cut a circle of wax or silicone paper the diameter of the pan base.

Cut a strip of paper about 1 inch longer than the circumference of the pan and 2 inches more than the depth. Make a fold along one long edge of the strip and cut slits in the fold about $\frac{1}{2}$ inch deep and 1 inch apart.

Press the strip around the sides of the pan so that the folded cut edge overlaps the pan base. Place the circle of paper in the base to hold the overlap in place.

To keep the cake moist and prevent it from sticking, brush the paper with shortening.

For a large loaf pan: cut a strip of wax paper 13 X 5 inches. Grease the pan. Press the paper into the bottom of the pan and smooth it up the long sides, leaving 1 inch above the pan on either side. Cut another strip of wax paper 17 X 9 inches and press it in the same way into the bottom and up the short sides of the pan.

Raisin Spice Cake

1 cup raisins
1 cup coarsely chopped walnuts
1 cup boiling water
1 teaspoon baking soda
$1\frac{1}{2}$ cups flour
$\frac{1}{4}$ teaspoon salt
$\frac{1}{2}$ cup butter or shortening
1 teaspoon vanilla
1 teaspoon lemon juice
1 cup sugar
1 egg
2 egg yolks
1 teaspoon ground cinnamon

Large loaf pan (9 X 5 X 3 inches)

Method
Line the pan and set the oven at moderately low (325°F).

Pour boiling water over the raisins and nuts, add the baking soda and let stand.

Sift the flour and salt. Cream the butter or shortening with the vanilla and lemon juice. Gradually add the sugar and beat until the mixture is light and fluffy.

Beat the egg and egg yolks with the cinnamon until slightly thick. Stir gradually into the butter and sugar mixture. Stir in raisin and nut mixture alternately with the flour, starting and ending with flour.

Spoon the cake batter into the prepared pan and bake in heated oven for $1\frac{1}{4}$ hours or until a skewer or toothpick inserted in the center comes out clean. Cool the cake in the pan for 30 minutes, then turn out onto a wire rack to cool completely. Cake keeps well for 1–2 weeks in an airtight container.

Simple Cherry Cake

1½ cups candied cherries
2 cups flour
⅔ cup butter
1½ cups sugar
4 eggs
1 teaspoon vanilla extract
⅔ cup commercial sour cream
confectioners' sugar (for
   sprinkling)

8 inch springform pan

Method

Grease the cake pan, sprinkle it with sugar, then with flour, discarding the excess.

Rinse the cherries in boiling water to wash away the syrup and dry thoroughly on paper towels. Set oven at low (300°F).

Toss the cherries with a little of the flour until well coated. Sift the remaining flour onto a piece of wax paper.

Cream the butter, beat in the sugar and continue beating until the mixture is soft and light. Beat in the eggs, one by one, and beat thoroughly after each addition. Stir in the vanilla. Add the flour alternately with the sour cream, folding it into the mixture with a metal spoon. Add the cherries with the last batch of flour.

When the batter is smooth, spoon it into the prepared pan and bake in the heated oven for 1¾–2 hours or until a skewer inserted in the center comes out clean. Let cool in the pan for 10 minutes before turning out the cake and transferring it to a wire rack to cool completely. Sprinkle generously with confectioners' sugar before serving.

Golden Fruit Cake

1 cup dried apricots
1 cup raisins
1 slice of candied pineapple, chopped
$\frac{1}{2}$ cup candied cherries, chopped
1 cup coarsely chopped walnuts
2 cups flour
$\frac{1}{2}$ teaspoon baking soda
$\frac{1}{2}$ teaspoon salt
$\frac{2}{3}$ cup butter
$\frac{2}{3}$ cup sugar
3 eggs, beaten to mix
grated rind of 1 lemon
grated rind of 1 orange
shredded almonds (to finish) – optional

Large loaf pan (9 X 5 X 3 inches)

Method
Line the pan and set oven at moderately low (325°F). Sift flour with baking soda and salt.

Cover the apricots with boiling water and soak 5 minutes or until soft. Drain and chop them coarsely.

Combine apricots, raisins, pineapple, cherries and walnuts and toss with $\frac{1}{4}$ cup of the flour until well coated.

Cream the butter, gradually add the sugar and beat until light and fluffy. Beat in the eggs a little at a time and continue beating for 1 minute. With a metal spoon fold in the remaining flour, one half at a time; fold in fruits and nuts with lemon and orange rind.

Spoon mixture into prepared pan, level top and scatter over shredded almonds, if you like. Bake in heated oven for $1\frac{1}{2}$ hours or until a skewer or toothpick inserted in the center comes out clean. Cool the cake in the pan for 30 minutes, then turn out onto a wire rack to cool completely.

Decorate golden fruit cake with shredded almonds, if you like

Golden Raisin and Cherry Cake

3 cups golden raisins
2 cups candied cherries, halved
2 cups flour
pinch of salt
$\frac{3}{4}$ cup butter
grated rind of $\frac{1}{2}$ lemon
$\frac{3}{4}$ cup sugar
4 eggs, beaten to mix

8 inch springform pan

Method
Line the pan and set the oven at moderate (350°F).

Sift the flour with the salt. Combine the golden raisins and cherries and toss with one-third of the flour until thoroughly coated.

Cream the butter with the lemon rind, add the sugar gradually and beat until the mixture is soft and fluffy. Beat in the eggs, a little at a time, beating well after each addition. Fold in half the remaining flour, the fruit mixture, then the last portion of flour.

Spoon the mixture into the prepared pan and bake in heated oven for 1 hour. Reduce heat to moderately low (325°F) and bake about 1 hour longer or until a skewer or toothpick inserted in the center comes out clean. Cool the cake in the pan for 30 minutes, then turn out onto a wire rack to cool completely.

If possible store the cake 1–2 weeks in an airtight container before eating.

Cherry and Walnut Cake

$\frac{3}{4}$ cup candied cherries, halved
$\frac{1}{2}$ cup coarsely chopped walnuts
$\frac{3}{4}$ cup butter
$\frac{3}{4}$ cup sugar
3 eggs, beaten to mix
2 cups self-rising flour
pinch of salt
1–2 tablespoons milk

7 inch springform pan

Method
Line the pan and set the oven at moderate (350°F).

Cream the butter, add the sugar gradually and beat until the mixture is light and fluffy. Beat in the eggs, a little at a time, beating well between each addition.

Sift the flour with the salt; mix 2 tablespoons of flour with the cherries and walnuts to coat them.

With a metal spoon, fold the remaining flour into the egg mixture one-third at a time, then fold in the cherries, walnuts and milk.

Spoon the mixture into the prepared pan and bake in heated oven for $1–1\frac{1}{4}$ hours or until a skewer or toothpick inserted in the center comes out clean. Cool the cake in the pan for 30 minutes, then turn out onto a wire rack to cool completely.

This cake keeps well for 1–2 weeks in an airtight container.

Fresh fruit cakes

Fresh fruit adds zest to a cake. Some fresh fruit cakes have fruit purée added to the batter, others are upside down cakes with whole pieces of fruit baked into the cake. All are good for desserts with a pleasantly tart fruit flavor and a rich, close texture.

Whole Orange Cake

1 large orange
1 cup golden raisins
$\frac{1}{2}$ cup coarsely chopped walnuts
1 cup milk
2 eggs
2 cups flour
1 teaspoon salt
1 teaspoon baking soda
$\frac{1}{2}$ cup butter
1 cup sugar

9 inch tube pan

Method

Grease the pan and set the oven at moderate (350°F).

Squeeze the orange juice and reserve. Put the peel (including white pith) in a blender with the milk and eggs and work at high speed until the peel is very finely chopped.

Sift the flour with the salt and baking soda.

Cream the butter, add the sugar and beat until soft and fluffy. Fold in the flour and orange rind mixture alternately; stir in the golden raisins and walnuts.

Pour the batter into the prepared pan and bake in the heated oven for 45–50 minutes or until the cake springs back when lightly pressed with a fingertip.

Sprinkle the reserved orange juice over the hot cake and leave in the pan until almost cool.

Fresh Strawberry Cake

1 pint of strawberries, hulled
$\frac{3}{4}$ cup butter
$\frac{3}{4}$ cup sugar
3 eggs, beaten to mix
$1\frac{1}{2}$ cups cake flour
pinch of salt
1 teaspoon baking powder
1 teaspoon vanilla
confectioners' sugar (for sprinkling)

8 inch springform pan

Method

Grease and flour the pan and set the oven at moderate (350°F).

In a bowl cream the butter, add the sugar gradually and beat until the mixture is light and fluffy. Beat in the eggs, a little at a time, beating thoroughly after each addition. Sift the flour with the salt and baking powder.

Cut the strawberries into 3–4 pieces — they should measure 2 cups. Toss them with a little of the flour mixture so they are thoroughly coated. Fold the rest of the flour into the egg mixture, then stir in the strawberries with the vanilla.

Transfer the batter to the prepared pan and bake in heated oven for 50–60 minutes or until the cake springs back when lightly pressed with a fingertip. Turn out the cake onto a wire rack to cool and sprinkle with confectioners' sugar.

Note: to appreciate the fresh strawberry flavor, eat this cake the day it is baked.

Pineapple Upside-Down Cake

For topping
1 fresh pineapple or 1 can (1 lb 4 oz) pineapple slices
6 tablespoons sugar
$\frac{1}{4}$ cup unsalted butter
6–8 candied cherries
6–8 walnut halves

For sugar syrup (if using fresh pineapple)
6 tablespoons sugar
$\frac{3}{4}$ cup water

For cake
$\frac{1}{2}$ cup butter
grated rind and juice of 1 orange
$\frac{1}{2}$ cup sugar
2 eggs, beaten to mix
$1\frac{1}{4}$ cups self-rising flour
pinch of salt

9 inch springform pan

Method

Grease sides of the pan only.

To make the topping: if using fresh pineapple, peel, slice and remove the core.

To make the sugar syrup: dissolve the sugar in the water in a large skillet. Add the fresh pineapple slices and cook very slowly until they look almost transparent.

Watchpoint: do not let the syrup boil hard or it will caramelize and change color.

Lift out the pineapple slices with a slotted spoon and drain them on a wire rack.

Add 6 tablespoons sugar to the skillet with the butter; heat gently until the sugar has dissolved and butter melted.

If using canned pineapple, drain it, reserving 2 tablespoons juice. Put 6 tablespoons sugar, butter and reserved juice into a pan and heat gently until the sugar has dissolved and the butter is melted.

Spoon the butter and sugar syrup mixture into the cake pan. Arrange the pineapple slices overlapping slightly in the pan and decorate the gaps with cherries and walnut halves.

Set the oven at moderate (350°F).

To make the cake: cream the butter with the grated orange rind, add the sugar and beat until light and fluffy. Beat in the eggs, a little at a time, and continue beating for 1 minute. Sift the flour with the salt and fold into the mixture alternately with the orange juice.

Spoon the cake mixture into the prepared pan and bake in heated oven for 45–50 minutes or until a skewer or toothpick inserted in the center comes out clean.

Turn the cake upside down onto a warm platter, but leave the pan on for a few minutes so the topping runs down over the cake.

Serve the cake warm with whipped cream or a hard sauce such as lemon or brandy.

Serve mouth-watering pineapple upside-down cake with a hard sauce or whipped cream

Upside-Down Apple Cake

For topping
4–5 dessert apples, pared
    cored and sliced
$\frac{1}{4}$ cup butter
$\frac{1}{4}$ cup sugar, or to taste
$\frac{1}{2}$ cup apricot jam glaze or
    confectioners' sugar (to
    finish)

For cake
$\frac{1}{2}$ cup butter
grated rind and juice of
    1 lemon
$\frac{1}{2}$ cup sugar
2 eggs, beaten to mix
$1\frac{1}{4}$ cups self-rising flour
pinch of salt

9 inch springform pan

Method
To make topping: spread half
the butter thickly over pan,
arrange a layer of apple in
bottom, sprinkle with sugar
and dot with butter.

Watchpoint: do not sprinkle
base of pan with sugar or the
mixture may caramelize and
stick.

    Continue adding layers of
apple with sugar and butter
until all are used. Set oven at
moderate (350°F).

    To make cake: cream
butter with grated lemon
rind, add sugar and beat until
mixture is light and fluffy.
Beat in eggs, one at a time,
and continue beating for 1
minute. Sift flour with salt and
fold it into the mixture alternately with lemon juice.

    Spoon mixture into pre-
pared pan and bake in heated
oven for 45–50 minutes or
until a skewer inserted in the
center comes out clean. Cool
in pan. Remove pan sides, turn
cake upside down onto a platter and remove pan base.
Brush top of cake with melted
apricot jam glaze or sprinkle
with confectioners' sugar.

Upside-down apple cake may be brushed with jam glaze or sprinkled with confectioners' sugar

Christmas Cakes

The traditional Christmas fruit cake should be made as far in advance as possible — the beginning of November is certainly not too early. Here are two dark fruit cake recipes, one fairly plain and the other rich. A lighter alternative is the white fruit cake on page 68.

Two simple but very attractive Christmas cakes are coated and decorated with royal icing. For the cake in front, pipe a lattice pattern on top, with a fine plain tube, and the rosettes with a small star tube, then top with silvered sugar balls called dragées. For cake at back roughen the icing to peaks on top and pipe shell border with a shell tube

Christmas Cake

3 cups golden raisins
2 cups raisins
1 cup candied cherries, halved
$\frac{1}{2}$ cup chopped candied peel
1 cup slivered almonds
2 cups flour
pinch of salt
$\frac{1}{2}$ teaspoon ground cinnamon
$\frac{1}{2}$ teaspoon ground nutmeg
$\frac{3}{4}$ cup butter
grated rind of $\frac{1}{2}$ lemon
   or orange
$\frac{3}{4}$ cup dark brown sugar
4 eggs, beaten to mix
2 tablespoons brandy, rum or
   sherry or 1 tablespoon
   orange juice

8 inch springform pan

Method
Line the pan with a double thickness of paper. Set oven at moderate (350°F).

Sift the flour with the salt and spices and divide the mixture into three. Mix one portion with the golden raisins, raisins, cherries, candied peel and almonds and toss well until thoroughly coated.

Cream the butter, add the lemon or orange rind and brown sugar and continue beating until the mixture is very soft. Beat in the eggs, a little at a time, and continue beating for 1 minute. With a metal spoon, fold in one portion of flour, then the flour and fruit mixture. Finally fold in the remaining flour with the brandy, rum, sherry or orange juice.

Spoon the cake mixture into the prepared pan and smooth the top. Dip your fingers or a pastry brush in water and moisten the surface very lightly. The small amount of steam from this water prevents the crust of the cake from hardening during the long baking.

Watchpoint: be sure there is only a thin film of water on the surface.

Put the cake in the center of the heated oven and bake 1 hour. Reduce heat to moderately low (325°F) and cover the top of the cake with foil or a double thickness of brown or silicone paper. Bake 1 hour longer or until a skewer or toothpick inserted in the center comes out clean.

Cool the cake in the pan for 30 minutes, then turn out onto a wire rack to cool completely.

Peel the paper lining from the cake, wrap the cake in wax paper or cheesecloth and store in an airtight container for at least 1 month before decorating. Sprinkle it from time to time during storage with a little extra brandy, rum or sherry to moisten it.

Rich Christmas Cake

3 cups golden raisins
3 cups raisins
2 cups currants
¾ cup finely chopped candied
　peel
¾ cup candied cherries, halved
1 cup slivered almonds
2½ cups flour
½ teaspoon salt
1 teaspoon baking soda
1 teaspoon ground cinnamon
1½ teaspoons ground allspice
¼ teaspoon ground cloves
¼ teaspoon ground nutmeg
2 squares (2 oz) sweet
　chocolate, cut up
1 cup butter
1 cup dark brown sugar
1 tablespoon molasses
6 eggs
6 tablespoons brandy, sherry,
　apple cider or orange juice

*9 inch springform pan or
10 inch tube pan*

Method
Line the pan with a double thickness of paper. Do not grease the inside paper as the cake mixture is very rich. Set oven at low (300°F).

Sift the flour, salt, baking soda and spices together and divide into three. Mix one portion with the raisins, currants, candied peel, cherries and almonds and toss to coat well.

Melt the chocolate on a heatproof plate over a pan of hot water and cool it slightly.

Cream the butter, gradually add the sugar and beat until very soft. Stir in the molasses. Beat in eggs, one at a time. Stir in a second portion of flour. Stir in the cool but still liquid chocolate with the fruit and nut mixture and the brandy, sherry, cider or orange juice. Stir in remaining portion of flour — if you like, use your hands for this.

Spoon the batter into the prepared pan, smooth the top with a spatula and brush it with a very little water — this helps to keep the cake soft on top during the long baking.

Bake the cake in heated oven for 1½ hours or until the cake is brown on top; cover it with foil, reduce the heat to 275°F and bake 1–1½ hours longer or until a skewer or toothpick inserted in the center comes out clean.

Cool the cake in the pan for 30 minutes, then turn out onto a wire rack to cool completely.

When the cake is cold, remove the paper lining, wrap in several layers of wax paper or cheesecloth and store in an airtight container for at least 1 month before using.
Note: to double this recipe, double all the ingredients and make the cake in the same way. Bake it in a 14 inch springform pan in a low oven (300°F) for 1½ hours, reduce heat to 275°F, cover cake with foil and bake 3½–3 hours longer or until it tests done. Cool and store as above.

White Fruit Cake

1½ cups golden raisins
½ cup chopped candied citron
　peel
½ cup chopped candied orange
　peel
½ cup chopped candied lemon
　peel
½ cup candied cherries
½ cup chopped candied
　pineapple
2 cups whole blanched
　almonds
2 cups flour
1 teaspoon baking powder
pinch of salt
½ cup butter
1 cup sugar
4 eggs, separated
½ cup white wine

9 inch springform pan

Method
Line the pan with a double thickness of paper. Set oven at low (300°F).

Sift the flour with the baking powder and salt and divide it into three. Mix one portion with the golden raisins, candied peel, cherries, pineapple and almonds and toss so the fruit is well coated.

Cream the butter, gradually beat in the sugar and continue beating until the mixture is light and fluffy. Add the egg yolks one at a time, beating well between each addition. Fold in one portion of the flour with half the white wine, stir in the fruit mixture, then fold in the remaining flour with the remaining wine.

Beat the egg whites until they hold a stiff peak and with a metal spoon fold into the batter as lightly as possible.

Spoon the batter into the prepared pan and smooth the top. Brush lightly with water to prevent the top from hardening during the long baking and bake in heated oven for 2–2½ hours or until a skewer or toothpick inserted in the center comes out clean.

After 1 hour, or when the top is brown, cover the cake with a piece of foil to prevent further browning. Cool the cake in the pan for 30 minutes, then turn out onto a wire rack to cool completely.

Remove the lining paper, wrap in wax paper or cheesecloth and store in an airtight container for at least 1 month before using.

To Age Fruit Cakes

Wrap the cake in cheesecloth soaked in rum, sherry or brandy and place in a crock or large kettle that has a tight-fitting lid. Add 1–2 apples, cut in half, and cover tightly. Check on the cake about once a week and, as the cheesecloth dries out, sprinkle a little more spirits over the cloth to keep the cake moist. The cake should age at least 1 month.

Decorating Christmas Cakes

The decoration is half the fun of a Christmas cake. Whether you choose familiar boiled frosting or go to the trouble of making crisp royal icing and piping elaborate decorations, a snowy white or pale pink coating adds immeasurably to the festive appearance of the cake. For a simple decoration, cover the top of the cake with almond paste, then coat this with milk or glacé icing so the icing covers the almond paste completely. Quickly press halved candied cherries around the icing at the side of the cake and decorate the top with a few more cherries.

Points to remember

1 The top surface of fruit cakes is seldom smooth so a good trick is to turn the cake upside down before coating it with icing. If you brush the surface with hot apricot jam glaze and leave the glaze to set, the icing will spread more evenly and crumbs will not get into the icing.

2 You may like to follow the English custom of coating a fruit cake with a layer of almond paste before adding an icing. This not only provides a flat surface for spreading the icing, but also adds moisture and flavor to the cake. Cover the cake with almond paste about 1 week before adding the final icing as the paste needs time to dry and harden.

3 Royal icing is used for the most elaborate decorations, like those done by professional bakers. The icing itself is easy to make and the skill lies in spreading it over the cake so it

is completely smooth; it is then left to harden. Unlike most icings, royal icing hardens slowly, so it can be shaped and worked to obtain a really smooth finish.

Two or even three layers of icing may be needed before the decoration is added. Simple designs can be done all at once, but more fancy ones must be carried out in stages, like the icing layers. Royal icing keeps well, so you can start to decorate the cake 1 week or more in advance.

4 Milk icing is soft and glossy; it is tricky to make and needs careful handling but takes much less time than royal icing and many people prefer the softer texture. A coating of milk icing will hold up well for several days.

5 Glacé icing is quick and easy to make but tends to crack on standing. It should be kept as short as possible.

6 Boiled frosting is also simple to make, providing the sugar syrup is boiled to just the right temperature. It has an attractive, rough-textured surface which can be molded in peaks or swirls, as you like. It keeps well for up to 2 days, then tends to separate slightly.

Almond Paste

5 cups whole almonds, blanched and ground
1½ cups confectioners' sugar
2 cups granulated sugar
2 eggs
2 egg yolks
juice of 1 lemon
2 tablespoons brandy, rum or sherry
1 teaspoon vanilla
3 tablespoons orange flower water (from specialty stores and some pharmacies) or orange juice

Makes about 3 lb almond paste or enough to cover the top and sides of a 9–10 inch cake. Leftover almond paste trimmings can be used for stuffing pitted dates.

Method

Sift the confectioners' sugar into a bowl and combine with the almonds and granulated sugar. Beat the eggs, egg yolks, lemon juice and flavorings until mixed, add to the almonds and sugar and stir until mixed. Knead to form a smooth paste.

Almond paste should be very smooth and pliable without being sticky. The mixture is dry at first but works to a paste when oil is drawn out of almonds during kneading.

Cake Boards

Professional bakers mount cakes on cardboard circles covered with foil to provide a firm foundation and make decorating easier. You can buy these at bakery supply houses or make one by covering a firm piece of cardboard with foil.

The board can be 2–4 inches larger than the cake, depending on the thickness of the coating icing, so that a border of 1–1½ inches will show around the finished cake.

Or if you prefer the board to be invisible, select a thin board the same size as the cake and cover it with icing.

Either way, the finished cake is best displayed on a stand or silver tray.

To Color and Flavor Icing

Edible food coloring enables you to tint icing all colors of the rainbow. You can make 5 color changes from 1 bowl of icing by going from white to yellow, to pink or green, to coffee or chocolate.

Improve the whiteness of royal icing by adding a tiny drop of blue color. Beat it in very thoroughly — too much blue gives the icing a grayish tint. About 1–2 teaspoons glycerine added to royal icing prevents it from becoming excessively hard as it dries.

Many flavoring extracts are available, and you can also use instant coffee or cocoa dissolved in a little water, or melted chocolate, or rum and fruit liqueurs. A squeeze of lemon or orange juice helps to balance the sweetness of icing.

Watchpoint: take great care when adding a color or flavor to icing because an extra drop of color can change a subtle shade to a gaudy one, and an extra drop of flavoring can spoil a cake's flavor.

Sprinkle the board and rolling pin with granulated sugar to prevent the paste from sticking. Divide the paste in half; roll one-half into a circle the size of the cake.

Brush the top of the cake with melted apricot jam glaze. Set the cake upside down on top of the paste and, with your left hand firmly on the cake, rotate it gently and cut and mold the paste level with this top edge. Turn the cake right side up and brush away any crumbs.

Shape remaining paste into a long roll and roll out with the rolling pin to a strip the circumference and depth of the cake. Trim the edges of the paste, then brush it with hot apricot jam glaze. Roll this strip around the cake, glazed side next to it. Make a neat join and smooth the surface by rolling it firmly with a straight-sided bottle or rolling pin. Leave about 1 week to harden.

To Decorate Rose Cake

Equipment needed for decorating 'rose' cake, left and pages 72–73, is as follows: straight-edge metal ruler or long metal spatula; plastic scraper or piece of stiff cardboard; cake board or cardboard covered with foil; turntable (optional); decorating nail (or round dial of a meat thermometer); fine plain tube; medium slanting petal tube; small star tube; medium leaf tube; wax paper decorating cones (see Volume 2).

For a charming Christmas or birthday cake, decorate the sides with royal icing rose garlands and top with a bouquet of fresh flowers or with more icing roses, as you like. The coating icing may be left white or tinted delicate pink as shown here

Royal Icing

3½ cups (1 lb) confectioners'
   sugar
2 egg whites
1 teaspoon lemon juice
1–2 teaspoons glycerine
food coloring (to taste)

Glycerine is available at pharmacies. This icing is too hard for sponge cakes and other cakes with a soft crumb. Makes 2–2½ cups icing or enough to coat the top and sides of a 9–10 inch cake.

Method
Sift the confectioners' sugar. Beat the egg whites until frothy and beat in the confectioners' sugar 1 tablespoon at a time. Continue beating until the mixture stands in peaks. Add the lemon juice, glycerine, and color as you like.
Watchpoint: keep the bowl of icing covered with a damp cloth while using as icing tends to dry on the surface.

If necessary, add a little more sugar or egg white to make a mixture that is stiff but spreads easily.

To use Royal Icing

Put the cake on a foil-covered cake board and set this on a revolving turntable or on an upturned bowl so the cake can be turned easily.

Spread the icing roughly in a thick layer over the top of the cake and work well to remove any air bubbles.

Place a plastic or metal ruler with a straight edge, or a long metal spatula, on the edge of the cake furthest away from you at an angle of 45° to the cake. Pull the ruler or knife across the top in one continuous movement to prevent bumps and holes from forming. Repeat pulling the ruler or knife back and forth until the top is really smooth. Trim excess icing that has gone over the sides of the cake with a metal spatula and let dry several hours. With a metal spatula, coat the sides of the cake generously with more icing.

To smooth the surface, hold a plastic scraper or piece of stiff cardboard at an angle of 45° to the cake; with your left hand at the front of the board pull the cake around, turning it in 1 or 2 complete circles until the icing is smooth; lift off the spatula. Repeat if necessary. Trim any excess icing from the top of the cake so the edge is sharp and let dry at least 24 hours before decorating.

Milk Icing

½ cup milk
1 teaspoon butter
1½ cups sugar
flavoring and food coloring
   (to taste)

Sugar thermometer

Makes about 1 cup icing or enough to cover the top and sides of a 9 inch cake.

Method
Melt the butter in a saucepan, add the sugar and milk and cook, stirring, until the mixture comes to a boil. Boil, without stirring, until the mixture spins a thread when a little is lifted on a teaspoon and tested between finger and thumb (230°F–234°F on a sugar thermometer).

Cool the mixture until hot to the touch, then beat until the icing reaches the right spreading consistency. Add flavoring and coloring to taste and pour over the cake, spreading evenly with a spatula.
Watchpoint: this is a tricky icing and it may harden before you are able to spread it on the cake. If this happens, place the pan over hot water, melt the icing and beat it a second time. Usually with this second beating, the icing stays at the proper consistency.

Glacé Icing

2 cups confectioners' sugar
flavoring and food coloring
   (to taste)

For sugar syrup
¼ cup sugar
½ cup water

Makes 1½ cups icing or enough to coat the top and sides of a 9 inch cake.

Method
To make the sugar syrup: dissolve the sugar in the water over low heat, bring to a boil and simmer 4–5 minutes.

Take the pan from the heat and when cold beat in the confectioners' sugar a tablespoon at a time. Let the pan stand in a pan of hot water until lukewarm. The icing should coat the back of a spoon, but still pour easily; add more confectioners' sugar or sugar syrup until it is the right consistency. Add flavoring and coloring.

Pour the icing at once over the cake and spread it evenly with a metal spatula.

Boiled Frosting

2 cups sugar
1 cup water
pinch of cream of tartar,
   dissolved in 1 teaspoon
   water
2 egg whites
food coloring and flavoring
   (to taste)

Sugar thermometer

Makes about 2 cups frosting or enough to coat the top and sides of a 9 inch cake.

Method
Put the sugar and water in a saucepan and dissolve, without stirring, over low heat. Add the dissolved cream of tartar to this syrup, cover the pan and bring to a boil. Boil 2 minutes, remove the lid, put the bulb of a sugar thermometer in the syrup and boil steadily to 238°F–240°F or until the syrup forms a soft ball when dropped in cold water.
Watchpoint: this temperature must be measured very accurately.

Meanwhile beat the egg whites until they hold a stiff peak.

Stop the boiling of the sugar syrup by dipping the bottom of the pan in cold water. Then, holding the pan well above the bowl of egg whites, pour in the syrup in a steady stream, beating constantly. Continue to beat until the frosting holds a peak and no longer looks glossy. Add food coloring and flavoring to taste.

Frost the cake at once, spreading the frosting quickly with a metal spatula. Finish the surface in uneven peaks or in swirls, as you like. Work fast as the frosting sets quickly.

ICING AND DECORATING A CHRISTMAS

1

1 *Prepare the almond paste and cover the top of the cake (see page 70 for detailed instructions). Roll out the strip for the sides, brush with apricot jam glaze and press the glazed side of the almond paste strip onto the sides of the cake. Smooth with a rolling pin or straight-sided bottle. Leave to harden for about 1 week*

2 *Spread royal icing in a thick layer on top of the cake with a metal spatula and work well to remove any air bubbles*

2

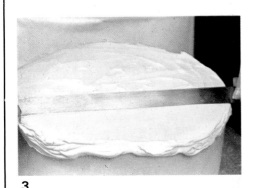

3

3 *Hold a metal ruler or spatula at a 45° angle and pull it back and forth across the cake until the surface is smooth. Trim excess icing from the sides of the cake. Leave icing to harden for several hours*

4 *Place the cake (still on the cake board) on a turntable or upturned bowl; spread extra icing down the side. Hold a plastic scraper or piece of stiff cardboard at a 45° angle; rotate the board until the sides of the cake are smooth. Spread a thin layer of icing on the flat surface of the board*

4

CAKE

5

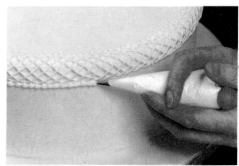

6

5 *Place a fine plain tube in a paper decorating cone, fill it with icing and pipe diagonal lines around top edge of the cake at $\frac{1}{4}$ inch intervals, then pipe lines in the opposite direction to form a lattice. Pipe third and fourth lines of lattice on top of the original ones. Let each layer dry before applying the next*

6 *Using a paper decorating cone fitted with a small star tube, cover the edges of the lattice at the top and base of the cake with a small shell border*

7

8

7 *If decorating the top with roses (or buds) of icing, use a paper decorating cone fitted with a fine plain tube and dot the rim of a small glass or cup. Press these dots lightly onto the top of the cake to mark out the areas of 5 evenly spaced circles*

8 *With a paper decorating cone fitted with a fine plain tube, mark out 5 loops on the side of the cake, making 1 loop between each of the circles marked on top of the cake*

10

9

9 *Taking the dots on top of the cake and the loops on the side as guiding lines, arrange the flowers (or buds) as shown here and on the finished rose cake page 70. Attach each flower to the cake with a little icing pressed from the decorating cone. For instructions on making roses, see page 75.*

10 *With a paper decorating cone fitted with a medium leaf tube, pipe leaves between the flowers by holding the tube at an angle to the surface of the cake; press the cone with the thumb, then lift it away with a slight pull*

PIPED DECORATIONS

Few garnishes lend such a professional finish to a dish as piped decorations. For example, a shell border of mashed potato or a dessert topping of rosettes of whipped cream can transform the plainest dish.

Handling a pastry bag is not difficult if you seal the top of the bag between the thumb and the first finger of the right hand, leaving the remaining fingers free to press the mixture in the bag. The other hand can then guide the tube and bag.

A nylon or canvas pastry bag, with a plastic lining, can be used for all mixtures, but for royal icing it is more convenient to make a number of wax or silicone paper cones so that several tubes can be used at once and the cones discarded when empty. (Instructions for making a paper decorating cone were given in Volumes 2 and 7.)

In general, meringue, whipped cream and mashed potato are piped through fairly large tubes, butter cream frosting through medium ones, and royal icing through small ones. The same-shaped tubes are available in different sizes, therefore the patterns you can create with different mixtures are similar in design but vary in scale.

The most versatile mixture is royal icing, which can be colored and shaped into a huge variety of flowers, patterns and geometric designs.

Butter cream frosting is almost as adaptable although less durable than royal icing.

Meringue, whipped cream and mashed potato are almost always piped through a star tube to form rosettes, twists and rope borders. Whipped cream needs careful handling because when very stiffly whipped, it can curdle when forced through a tube; once piped, refrigerate until serving time.

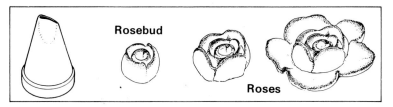

Rosebud

Roses

Slanting petal tube: makes rosebuds and roses (see rose cake on page 70) and other flowers.

Use for piping royal icing and butter cream frosting.

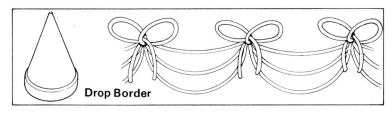

Drop Border

Fine plain tube: makes a lattice (see Christmas cake on page 67), a drop border with bows, and writing.

Use for piping royal icing and butter cream frosting.

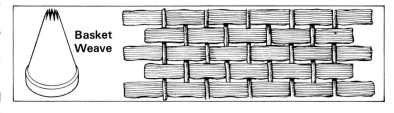

Basket Weave

Shell tube: makes a shell border (see Christmas cake at back, page 67) and a basket weave pattern (using medium plain tube for vertical lines).

Use for piping royal icing and butter cream frosting.

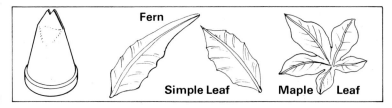

Fern

Simple Leaf

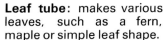

Maple Leaf

Leaf tube: makes various leaves, such as a fern, maple or simple leaf shape.

Use for piping royal icing and butter cream frosting.

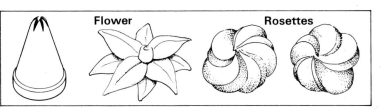

Flower

Rosettes

Star tube: makes flowers, rosettes, shell borders, and coil, rope or loop borders.

Use for piping royal icing, butter cream frosting, meringue, whipped cream and mashed potato.

TO PIPE ROSES

1 *Make 2–2½ cup quantity of royal icing and color about one-eighth of it bright pink. Fit a medium slanting petal tube into a paper decorating cone.*

Spread some of the pink icing down the side of the cone to the thin end of the tube opening; lay a knife over this, fill the cone with white royal icing and remove the knife.

Fold over the end of the cone to seal it and turn the cone so that the thick end of the tube is pointing down

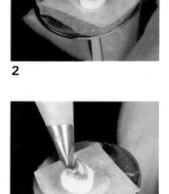

2 *Attach a 1 inch square of wax paper to a decorating nail (or you can use the round dial on a meat thermometer) with a little icing. Pipe a few circles of icing onto the wax paper to form the flower center*

3 *Pipe 2 more petals onto the flower center, still with the thick end of the tube down. This will form a bud*

4 *To make a medium-sized flower, add 3 more petals. Make about 10 buds and 20 medium flowers for a 9–10 inch cake (as shown on page 70). For a larger cake, about 14 inches diameter, you will need about 4 times this number if you want to decorate both the top and the sides of the cake with icing roses*

5 *To make larger flowers: pipe 5 petals onto medium flowers. Let the flowers dry 24 hours before removing the paper. You will need 5 large flowers for a small cake and 15 for a large one*

Garnish fried liver with browned orange slices (recipe is on page 78)

VARIETY MEATS (1)

Variety meats include the edible internal parts of an animal such as the liver and kidneys, as well as the head, tail and feet. This wide category provides something for everyone and covers such delicacies as sweetbreads and calf's liver, soul food like tripe and hearty recipes like oxtail stew and pigs' feet. The preparation of tongue, brains and sweetbreads will be covered in a future Volume.

The ·quality of variety meats varies because to be at their best they should be eaten very fresh — within 1–2 days. Often they are frozen but this tends to destroy their delicate flavor.

When carefully cooked, variety meats offer a rewarding choice of rich, unusual dishes, many of them expensive. Unfortunately, with the exception of fish, few foods are more maltreated and, as a result, they have acquired a reputation for being unappetizing. If cooked too fast or for too short or long a time (depending on the type of meat), they can easily become rubbery instead of moist and tender.

Points to remember

Liver

This is the most popular variety meat. Calf's liver has the most delicate flavor when fried; lamb's liver is also good fried, but pig's liver has a more pronounced flavor and is best added to stuffings, pâtés and terrines. Beef liver is not as delicate in flavor or texture as lamb's or calf's liver. Chicken livers make a delicious and economical dish.

All liver should be fresh and clean-looking, with little or no odor. Some calf's liver is slightly pale but this makes no difference in cooking.

The usual way to cook liver is to slice and fry it with bacon or onions, but it can also be braised as one piece, then sliced for serving with the gravy from cooking.

Kidneys

They are often broiled or they may be sautéed and served with a sauce. Veal kidneys are a delicacy; 1 kidney, weighing between 6–12 oz serves 1 person. To prepare, skin the kidney, if necessary, and with scissors snip away as much of the core as possible without cutting the kidney apart. After trimming, cut it in $\frac{1}{2}-\frac{3}{4}$ inch slices.

Lambs' kidneys also have a delicate flavor. Like pigs' kidneys, they are bean-shaped and $1\frac{1}{2}-2$ are needed for each serving. To skin them, slit the rounded side and draw the skin back towards the core. Pull this gently to draw out as much of the core as possible and cut the ducts with scissors. Cut the kidney open and remove the rest of the core. For broiling, the kidney may be split open and skewered flat; for a sauté or stew, cut it com-

pletely in half.

Pigs' kidneys may be broiled or sautéed like lambs' and veal kidneys, but they are usually best treated like beef kidneys because they have a strong flavor.

Beef kidneys are sometimes mixed with steak to use in pies or they can be braised or stewed. Before preparing them in the same way as veal kidneys, soak in warm salted water for 1 hour to remove any strong flavor. Beef kidneys are sold by the pound, and 1 lb serves 2–3 people.

Hearts

These are inexpensive but tend to be tasteless, so stuff lambs' hearts with a well-flavored herb stuffing, then braise them until very tender. Veal or pigs' hearts can be prepared in the same way but they must be cooked very slowly for a long time to make them tender. Beef heart is very large, tough and almost inedible. Allow 1 lamb's heart per person; 1 pig's or veal heart will serve 1–2 people, depending on size.

Tripe

This is the lining of beef stomach and can be delicious when it is correctly cooked. It has always been a popular country-style dish in France where it is fried or slowly braised à la mode de Caen (tripe braised on a bed of vegetables, in cider or water and Calvados). With the popularity of soul food it has become much more widely known here.

There are four kinds of tripe and they must all be prepared before cooking: trim the tripe, wash it thoroughly, soak it overnight in

cold water, then blanch in salted water for 15 minutes and drain; 1 lb tripe serves 2–3 people.

Chitterlings

These are the small intestines of a young pig. They can be stewed or braised or they can be simmered until tender and then sautéed in butter or deep fried. In France chitterlings are used to make a popular sausage called 'andouillettes'.

Soak them for 24 hours in several changes of water before using; 1 lb serves 2–3 people.

Oxtail

This makes excellent, hearty dishes — it is usually braised or simmered for a rich soup. A good oxtail has an equal amount of meat and bone, with white fat and bright red meat. An average tail will serve 3 people. For cooking, it should be divided into pieces through the joints.

Feet

These are full of gelatin and are often used for aspics and dishes where stock must set to a jelly. Calves' feet are particularly good and they have such a delicate flavor that they can be used for setting sweet as well as savory gelatins. Pigs' feet may be added to stock or to braised beef to give a rich gravy. They also make a rich hearty dish when baked, boiled, or braised.

To prepare calves' or pigs' feet, wash them thoroughly and split them open, cutting down between the toes and using a cleaver to cut through the bone at the base (the butcher will do this for you). Then blanch and drain thoroughly.

Fried Liver with Orange

8 slices of calf's liver or
  2 cups (1 lb) chicken livers
3 tablespoons flour, seasoned
  with little salt, pepper, dry
  mustard and cayenne
5 tablespoons butter
1 onion, finely sliced
2 cloves of garlic, crushed
$\frac{1}{3}$ cup red wine
$\frac{1}{3}$ cup well-flavored stock
1 tablespoon chopped parsley
$\frac{1}{2}$ teaspoon thyme

For pilaf
1 cup rice
2 tablespoons butter
1 onion, finely chopped
$2-2\frac{1}{2}$ cups veal or chicken stock
salt and pepper
2 tablespoons grated
  Parmesan cheese

For garnish
1 navel orange, unpeeled and
  cut in thin slices
2 tablespoons butter
1 tablespoon sugar

Method

To prepare the pilaf: melt $1\frac{1}{2}$ tablespoons butter in a flame-proof casserole, add the onion, cover and cook gently until soft but not browned. Add the rice and continue cooking, stirring, for 2–3 minutes or until the rice looks transparent. Add 2 cups stock, season and bring to a boil. Cover and cook in a moderate oven (350°F) for 15 minutes.

Add a little more stock if the pan is dry and cook 5–7 minutes longer until the rice is tender. Cool pilaf a little, then stir in the remaining butter and cheese with a fork.

Sprinkle the liver with the seasoned flour. Heat 2 tablespoons butter in a skillet and quickly sauté the liver for 3 minutes on each side or until lightly browned. Arrange on a platter and keep warm.

Some of the raw ingredients used for making fried liver with orange

Melt the remaining butter in the skillet, add the onion and garlic and cook until the onion is brown. Add the wine, stock and herbs and simmer 1 minute. Pour the sauce over the liver.

To prepare the garnish: heat the butter in a skillet, sprinkle the orange slices with sugar and brown them quickly on both sides in the butter.

Garnish the liver with the orange slices and serve the pilaf separately.

Liver and Bacon

$1\frac{1}{2}$ lb calf's or lamb's liver,
    cut in $\frac{1}{4}-\frac{1}{2}$ inch slices
$\frac{1}{2}$ lb sliced bacon
$\frac{1}{4}$ cup seasoned flour (made
    with $\frac{1}{4}$ teaspoon salt, pinch
    of pepper)
$\frac{3}{4}$ cup beef stock

Method

In a skillet fry the bacon until crisp, drain on paper towels and keep warm. Discard all but 2 tablespoons fat from the pan.

Coat the liver lightly on both sides with seasoned flour and sauté it quickly for about 3 minutes on each side or until lightly browned. When done, pink juice will bubble on top of the liver — it should be slightly pink when cut because it becomes tough and dry when overcooked.

Arrange alternate slices of liver and bacon on a platter, beginning and ending with the bacon. Add the stock to the skillet, stir until the juices are dissolved and pour this gravy over the liver. Serve at once; if kept hot for even a short time after cooking, sautéed liver tends to dry and harden.

Braised Liver with Mushrooms

1½ lb piece of calf's or lamb's
    liver
1 cup white wine
salt and pepper
bouquet garni
1 medium onion, sliced
6–8 slices of bacon
⅓ cup butter
1 tablespoon flour
4 tomatoes, peeled, seeded
    and finely chopped
2 cups (½ lb) small mushrooms
2–3 tablespoons olive oil
3 shallots, very finely chopped

*Trussing needle and string or
    poultry pins*

Method

Mix the wine, seasoning, bouquet garni and onion together. Pour this marinade over the liver in a dish (not metal), cover and leave 1½–2 hours; turn and baste the liver 2–3 times.

Take the liver from the marinade and pat dry with paper towels; strain and reserve the marinade. Wrap the bacon around the liver and secure with a trussing needle and string or fasten with poultry pins.

In a flameproof casserole, heat half the butter and brown the liver on all sides. Remove it, keep warm, add the remaining butter, stir in the flour and cook until straw-colored. Add the tomatoes and strained marinade, bring to a boil, put in the liver, cover and braise in a moderate oven (350°F) for about 30 minutes.

Trim the mushrooms and fry them quickly in the olive oil for 1 minute. Add the shallots, lower the heat and cook 1–2 minutes until the shallots are soft.

Add the mushroom mixture to the casserole and braise 20–30 minutes longer or until the liver is very tender.

To serve, remove string or poultry pins and slice the liver, discarding the bacon. Replace the liver in the casserole or arrange it on a platter. Pour over the sauce and mushrooms and serve with mashed potatoes.

Deviled Pigs' Feet

4 pigs' feet, split and blanched
    (see page 78)
1 onion
1 carrot
6 peppercorns
bouquet garni
salt
3–4 tablespoons melted butter

For devil mixture
1 tablespoon Dijon-style
    mustard, or 1½ teaspoons
    prepared mustard
2 tablespoons soy sauce, or
    1 tablespoon Worcestershire
    sauce
1 tablespoon ketchup
black pepper, freshly ground
1 teaspoon sugar

Method

Put the pigs' feet in a large kettle with onion, carrot, peppercorns, bouquet garni, water to cover and a little salt. Cover, bring to a boil and simmer 2–2½ hours or until the bone seems loose and the skin is soft, not rubbery. Leave to cool in the liquid, then carefully remove the feet and chill.

Combine the ingredients for devil mixture and spread it over the feet. Place them on a broiler rack, brush with melted butter and broil until hot and very well browned.

Serve on a bed of braised green cabbage, or cabbage Lorraine; serve boiled potatoes separately.

Cabbage Lorraine

1 firm head of green cabbage
1 medium onion, finely sliced
2–3 tablespoons olive oil or
    butter
4 tomatoes, peeled, seeded
    and sliced
salt and pepper
½ cup stock (optional)
1 cup sour cream or yogurt
1 tablespoon chopped parsley

Method

Set oven at moderate (350°F).

Trim the cabbage and put the whole head in a large pan of boiling salted water. Simmer 4–5 minutes. Drain, refresh and drain again, pressing the cabbage to remove all water. Cut the head in quarters and remove the hard stem. Tuck in the tips of the leaves and pack the quarters neatly into an ovenproof dish or casserole.

Cook the onion in the oil or butter until soft, add the tomatoes, season and cook 5 minutes or until the tomatoes are tender but not soft. Spoon the tomato mixture over the cabbage, cover the dish or casserole with foil, then the lid, and bake in the heated oven for 20–30 minutes or until the cabbage is tender. After the first 6–7 minutes, add a little of the stock if the mixture looks dry. This depends on the cabbage – if it is really fresh the juice from the tomatoes will be enough.

When the cabbage is tender, spoon the sour cream or yogurt over the top. Return the dish or casserole to the oven for 4–5 minutes to reheat thoroughly. Sprinkle with chopped parsley before serving.

Braised Oxtail

1 large or 2 small oxtails,
    cut at the joints
2 tablespoons oil
2 onions, quartered
2 carrots, quartered
3 stalks of celery, cut in
    2 inch lengths
1 tablespoon flour
2½–3 cups beef stock or water
bouquet garni
salt and pepper

Oxtail can be very fatty so, if possible, make the braise a day ahead, chill it overnight and skim off any fat that solidifies on top. Reheat for serving.

Method

In a large flameproof casserole heat the oil and brown the pieces of oxtail on all sides, a few at a time. Take out, add the onion, carrot and celery and brown lightly.

Take from the heat, sprinkle in the flour and add the stock or water. Bring to a boil, add the bouquet garni and seasoning and replace the oxtail.

Cover pot and braise in a moderately low oven (325°F) for 3–4 hours or until the oxtail meat falls easily from the bone. Remove bouquet garni, taste for seasoning and serve with mashed or boiled potatoes.

Salpicon is the name given to a mixture of ingredients which have been cut in shreds or strips. It may be served as a garnish, used as a stuffing for pastry cases and other dishes or made into croquettes. Often the mixture is bound with a rich white or brown sauce.

Cut the oxtail into pieces through the joints so it is manageable (or have your butcher do this)

Kidneys with Rice

For kidney salpicon
4 veal or 6–8 lambs' kidneys
3 tablespoons butter
1 small onion, finely chopped
1 cup (¼ lb) mushrooms
2 teaspoons flour
¼ cup sherry
1½ cups well-flavored stock
salt and pepper

For pilaf
1¼ cups rice
1 medium onion, chopped
2 tablespoons butter
1 tablespoon tomato paste
2½–3 cups well-flavored stock
1 tablespoon butter
1–2 tablespoons grated
  Parmesan cheese

Charlotte mold (5 cup capacity) or 7 inch springform pan

Method
To make the pilaf: in a flame-proof casserole fry the onion in butter until soft but not browned. Add rice and cook 2–3 minutes until the grains look transparent. Stir in the tomato paste, 2½ cups stock and seasoning, bring to a boil, cover and bake in moderate oven (350°F) for 15 minutes. If the pot is dry, add more stock and bake 5–7 minutes longer until the rice is tender and the stock is absorbed. Cool a little, then dot with the butter, sprinkle with cheese, cover and keep warm.

To prepare the salpicon: skin and split the kidneys in half lengthwise and cut out the cores. Cut the veal or lambs' kidneys into thick slices.

In a skillet, melt the butter, brown the kidneys quickly on both sides and remove. Add the onion and mushrooms and cook over medium heat until tender. Take from the heat, stir in the flour, add the sherry and stock and bring to a boil. Season, put back the kidneys, half cover the pan and simmer 20–25 minutes or until the kidneys are tender.

Generously butter the mold or springform pan.

Stir the pilaf with a fork, spoon it into the pan and press down lightly. Hollow the center slightly and put in a little of the kidney mixture without sauce. Unmold onto a deep platter and lift off the mold carefully. Spoon the remaining salpicon around the sides.

Alternatively the rice may be shaped in a 5 cup capacity ring mold, unmolded and the kidney salpicon spooned into the center.

Lambs' Kidneys Garibaldi

6–8 lambs' kidneys
3–4 tablespoons butter
6 tablespoons Marsala or
  sherry
2 medium onions, finely sliced
1 cup (¼ lb) quartered
  mushrooms
1 tablespoon flour
1 tablespoon tomato paste
1½ cups stock
1 bay leaf
1 clove of garlic, crushed
salt and pepper
4 tomatoes, peeled, seeded
  and sliced

Method
Skin and split the kidneys lengthwise and cut out the cores.

In a skillet heat the butter and fry the kidneys quickly on both sides until lightly browned. Heat the Marsala or sherry in a small pan, flame it and pour, flaming, over the kidneys. Take them out, add the onion and, after 1–2 minutes, add the mushrooms. Sauté until the mushrooms are tender, stir in the flour, tomato paste and stock and add the bay leaf, garlic and seasoning.

Put back the kidneys, half cover the pan and simmer 20–25 minutes or until the kidneys are tender. Add the tomatoes, heat thoroughly, remove the bay leaf, taste for seasoning and serve with saffron rice or mashed potatoes.

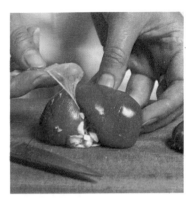
To prepare a kidney: first peel off the skin and then cut ducts with scissors

Split the kidney in half lengthwise and cut out any remaining core

Garibaldi was an Italian revolutionary who launched the campaign from Marsala in Sicily that led to the uniting of Italy under one flag. Marsala wine gives the characteristic flavor to this dish.

Kidneys Turbigo — with onions, sausages and mushrooms — are garnished with parsley and triangular fried croûtes of bread

Kidneys Turbigo

5–6 lambs' kidneys
12–18 baby onions
¼ cup butter
4–6 chipolata or country
 sausages
1 cup (¼ lb) quartered
 mushrooms
2 teaspoons flour
1 teaspoon tomato paste
1 tablespoon sherry
1 cup beef stock
1 bay leaf
salt and pepper
1 tablespoon chopped parsley
 (to serve)

For croûtes
2 slices of bread, crusts
 removed and cut in triangles
2–3 tablespoons oil and
 butter, mixed

Method
Blanch the onions, drain and
peel them. Skin the kidneys,
split them in half lengthwise
and cut out the cores.

In a sauté pan or skillet
heat the butter and sauté the
kidneys briskly, cut side down,
until brown on both sides.
Remove them, add the sausages, lower heat and brown
them all over. Take them out
and cut in half.

Add the onions and mush-
rooms to the pan and cook
over medium heat for 2–3
minutes or until the mushrooms are tender, shaking
the pan to prevent them from
sticking.

Take the pan from the heat,
discard all but 1 tablespoon
fat, and stir in the flour, tomato
paste, sherry and stock. Bring
to a boil, add the bay leaf,
seasoning, kidneys and sausages and cover pan. Simmer
20–25 minutes or until the
kidneys are tender. Remove
bay leaf.

Brown the croûtes in oil and
butter on both sides and drain
on paper towels.

Transfer the kidney mixture
to a deep platter, surround
with the croûtes and sprinkle
with chopped parsley before
serving.

Lambs' Kidneys with Herb Stuffing

8 lambs' kidneys
8 slices of bacon
bunch of watercress or slices
 of hot buttered toast (for
 garnish)

For herb stuffing
1½ tablespoons chopped
 parsley
1 teaspoon mixed herbs
 (thyme, basil, oregano) or
 1 teaspoon more parsley
¾ cup fresh white breadcrumbs
1 small onion, finely chopped
1½ tablespoons butter
salt and pepper
1 small egg, beaten to mix

8 toothpicks

Method
Skin the kidneys, slit them
two-thirds of the way through
and remove the cores but do
not halve them completely.

To make the stuffing: mix
the breadcrumbs and herbs
together. Cook the onion in
butter until soft, add to
the crumbs with seasoning
and bind the mixture together
with beaten egg. Fill this
stuffing into the kidneys and
wrap each with a slice of
bacon. Fasten with a toothpick.

Set the kidneys on a rack
in a roasting pan and bake in
a hot oven (400°F) for 8–
10 minutes. At the end of this
time the bacon should be
crisp, but if it is not, broil for a
few moments.

Serve the kidneys garnished
with watercress or on slices of
hot buttered toast.

Sautéed Chitterlings

2 lb chitterlings
1 tablespoon chopped parsley
1 lemon, cut in wedges (for
 garnish)

For simmering
2 onions, quartered
bouquet garni
2 cloves of garlic, sliced
½ teaspoon salt
10–12 peppercorns
juice of ½ lemon
1 quart water

For sautéing
½ cup seasoned flour (made
 with ½ teaspoon salt and
 pinch of pepper)
½ cup butter

Method
Soak the chitterlings in
several changes of water for
24 hours. Cut them in 2 inch
lengths and remove the
excess fat, leaving a little for
flavor. Put in a kettle with the
ingredients for simmering,
cover pan and simmer 2 hours
or until tender.

Watchpoint: do not boil the
the chitterlings or they will
become tough.

Drain the chitterlings thoroughly and toss with seasoned
flour until well coated.

In a large skillet melt
butter and briskly fry the
chitterlings, stirring occasionally, until browned all over.
Transfer them to a platter,
sprinkle with chopped parsley
and garnish with lemon wedges.

Tripe Italian Style

1½–2 lb fresh tripe, washed,
 soaked and blanched
 (see page 78)
1½ cups milk
2 cups water
salt and pepper
1 large onion, sliced
6 tablespoons olive oil
½ cup (2 oz) finely chopped
 mushrooms
1 bay leaf
3 tomatoes, peeled, seeded and
 finely chopped, or ¼ cup
 tomato purée
1 clove of garlic, crushed
¾ cup white wine
1 tablespoon chopped parsley
pinch of rosemary or oregano
pinch of ground nutmeg
¾–1 cup stock or water

Method
Put the prepared tripe in a
pan with the milk, water and
½ teaspoon salt, cover and
simmer 1 hour. Drain and cut
in fine strips 3½–4 inches long.

In a flameproof casserole
fry the onion in oil until it
begins to brown. Add the
mushrooms and cook 1
minute. Put in the tripe with
bay leaf, tomatoes or tomato
purée, garlic, wine, herbs,
nutmeg, stock or water and
seasoning. Cover the pot and
simmer 1 hour or until the tripe
is very tender. Remove bay
leaf and taste for seasoning.

Watchpoint: the tripe must
always be cooked very gently
or it will become tough and
rubbery.

If the mixture looks dry,
add some of the extra stock or
water from time to time during
cooking – the finished consistency should be thick and
rich. Serve with boiled potatoes.

Fillet of beef Italienne is served with gnocchi romana (recipes are on page 87)

Fillet of Beef is a superb entrée

Just as this fillet of beef proves that Italian cuisine means more than pasta and tomatoes, a bottle of Barolo should disprove any who still believe that Italian wines are limited to Chianti. Barolo is a rich, sophisticated wine that is unsurpassed in Italian viniculture. There is no exact equivalent in America, but a well-made Charbono from the San Francisco Bay area will be a suitable accompaniment to this dish.

If you choose the veal, a somewhat lighter red wine is called for and, continuing in the Italian vein, a happy choice would be the fragrant, fruity Valpolicella. For an American alternative, you might try the Californian Grignolino, usually somewhat sharper than Valpolicella.

Smoked Salmon Rolls with Shrimps

Fillet of Beef Italienne
Gnocchi Romana   Green Beans
or
Paupiettes de Veau Citronnées
Vichy Carrots   Tomato & Orange Salad

Hazelnut Meringue Cake
with Melba Sauce
~

Red wine (with Beef) — Barolo (Italy)
or Charbono (California)
Red wine (with Veal) — Valpolicella (Italy)
or Grignolino (California)

TIMETABLE

Day before
Bake meringue layers but do not fill.
Make Espagnole sauce for fillet of beef, cover and chill.
Prepare gnocchi, spread on tray or shallow baking sheet, cover and refrigerate.

Morning
Prepare green beans *or carrots; peel potatoes and keep in cold water.* Make salmon rolls, cover securely with plastic wrap and refrigerate; cut lemon wedges, wrap in plastic wrap and refrigerate; butter thin slices of brown bread, cover securely and refrigerate.
Prepare Melba sauce, cover and chill. *Stuff and roll escalopes of veal ready for cooking.*
Make sauce for gnocchi; cut out gnocchi, arrange in dish, add sauce and cheese, cover and refrigerate.
Sandwich meringue layers with whipped cream and raspberries; refrigerate.

Assemble equipment for final cooking from 7 p.m. for dinner around 8 p.m.

You will find that **cooking times** given in the individual recipes for these dishes have sometimes been adapted in the timetable to help you when cooking and serving this menu as a party meal.

Order of Work

7:00
Set oven at hot (400°F) for gnocchi.
Decorate top of hazelnut meringue cake.

7:10
Start cooking fillet of beef *or escalopes of veal.*

7:15
Cook green beans *or carrots.*
Boil potatoes.

7:30
Bake gnocchi.
Prepare tomato and orange salad.

7:40
Turn oven to low (300°F) and keep gnocchi warm.
Transfer beef *or veal* to platter and keep warm.
Mash potatoes and keep warm.
Complete the sauce for the beef *or veal* and keep warm.

8:00
Serve appetizer.
Toss green beans *or carrots* in butter to reheat them.
Arrange beef *or veal* on platters with accompaniments just before serving.

Appetizer

Smoked Salmon Rolls with Shrimps

12–14 thin slices (¾ lb) smoked salmon
¾ lb peeled, cooked shrimps, coarsely chopped
¾ cup mayonnaise
3–4 drops of Tabasco
½ teaspoon paprika
½ teaspoon tomato paste
1 tablespoon heavy cream

To serve
12–14 wedges of lemon
thin slices of buttered wholewheat bread

Method
In a bowl combine the mayonnaise with Tabasco, paprika, tomato paste and cream. Stir in the shrimps, and spoon some of this mixture in the center of each slice of salmon. Roll the slices with 2 forks and arrange on individual plates with a wedge of lemon at the side.
Serve the salmon rolls with thin slices of buttered wholewheat bread.

Serve the smoked salmon rolls with lemon wedges and thin slices of wholewheat bread

Use two forks to roll up the smoked salmon with shrimp and mayonnaise filling

The feature in this Volume on **Menus for the Weekend** suggests this menu for Saturday dinner (see page 96).
All recipes on pages 84–91 serve 6 people.

Entrée

Fillet of Beef Italienne

3 lb fillet of beef
2 tablespoons butter
1 onion, quartered
1 carrot, quartered
bouquet garni
1 tablespoon chopped parsley
2 thin slices of cooked ham,
   cut in strips

For sauce
1 cup ($\frac{1}{4}$ lb) mushrooms, sliced
2 tablespoons butter
2 shallots, finely chopped
$\frac{3}{4}$ cup white wine
1$\frac{1}{2}$ cups espagnole sauce
2 teaspoons tomato paste

Method

To make the sauce: sauté the mushrooms in butter for 2–3 minutes or until soft; remove and reserve. Stir the shallot and wine into the pan and cook the mixture until reduced by half. Add espagnole sauce and tomato paste, bring to a boil and simmer 3–4 minutes or until glossy and slightly thickened. Cover and reserve.

In a flameproof casserole, brown the beef well on all sides in the butter, remove and brown the onion and carrot. Pour off any fat, add bouquet garni and sauce and replace the meat. Cover the pot tightly and simmer on top of the stove 20–25 minutes (7 minutes per lb), turning the beef once or twice. The meat should be rare when cooked (a meat thermometer inserted in the center should register 140°F).

Strain the sauce, taste for seasoning and spoon over the meat. Add the mushrooms, parsley and ham to the pot

with the meat and reheat thoroughly. Serve with green beans and gnocchi romana.

Add the cooked mushrooms, chopped parsley and finely sliced ham to the cooked fillet of beef in the casserole

Espagnole Sauce

3 tablespoons oil
2 tablespoons finely diced
   onion
2 tablespoons finely diced
   carrot
1 tablespoon finely diced celery
1$\frac{1}{2}$ tablespoons flour
1 teaspoon tomato paste
1 tablespoon chopped
   mushrooms
2$\frac{1}{2}$ cups well-flavored brown
   stock
bouquet garni
salt and pepper

Makes about 1$\frac{1}{2}$ cups.

Method

In a saucepan, heat oil and add diced vegetables. Lower heat and cook gently until vegetables are transparent and about to brown. They will shrink slightly at this point.

Stir in the flour and brown it slowly, stirring constantly with a wire whisk or metal spoon and scraping the flour

well from the bottom of the pan. When it is brown, take from heat and cool slightly.
Watchpoint: the flour should be cooked until dark brown, but do not let it burn.

Stir in the tomato paste, chopped mushrooms, 2 cups cold stock, bouquet garni and seasoning. Bring to a boil, whisking constantly, partly cover pan and cook gently for 35–40 minutes. Skim off any scum that rises to the surface. Then add half the remaining stock, bring again to a boil and skim. Simmer 5 minutes, add remaining stock, bring to a boil and skim again. (The addition of cold stock accelerates the rising of scum.)

Cook 5 minutes longer, then strain, pressing vegetables gently to extract any juice. Clean pan and return sauce to it. Partly cover pan and continue to simmer sauce until it is very glossy and the consistency of heavy cream.

Accompaniment to entrée

Gnocchi Romana

1 cup cornmeal or coarse
   semolina
1 medium onion
1 bay leaf
2 cups milk
2 cups water
salt and pepper
1 teaspoon Dijon-style mustard
6 tablespoons butter
3 egg yolks
1 cup grated Parmesan or
   Romano cheese
mornay sauce (made with
   2 tablespoons butter,
   2 tablespoons flour, 2 cups
   milk, 2 egg yolks, $\frac{1}{4}$ cup
   grated Parmesan cheese)

Method

Put the onion, bay leaf, milk and water in a large saucepan, cover, bring to a boil and infuse 10 minutes. Discard the onion and bay leaf.

Stir the cornmeal or semolina into the seasoned milk mixture, bring to a boil, stirring, season and simmer, stirring often, for 7–10 minutes. The mixture should drop fairly easily from the spoon and not be sticky. If too thick, add more liquid.
Watchpoint: the amount of milk and water needed varies according to the type and coarseness of the grain used.

Take from the heat, stir in the mustard, half the butter, egg yolks and three-quarters of grated cheese; adjust seasoning. Pour the mixture onto a buttered tray or shallow baking sheet and spread it out to $\frac{1}{2}$–$\frac{3}{4}$ inch thickness. Cover and let stand for 2–3 hours in the refrigerator or overnight until firm.

Warm the tray lightly to melt the butter, turn the gnocchi onto a flat surface and cut into small squares, rounds or crescents. Arrange these in a large, well-buttered ovenproof dish with the pieces overlapping, leaving a slight well in the center. Sprinkle the gnocchi generously with the remaining butter, melted.

Spoon mornay sauce into the center of the dish and sprinkle with the remaining cheese. Bake in a hot oven (400°F) for 10–15 minutes or until brown.

Rolled escalopes of veal with lemon are served on a bed of mashed potato and garnished with baby carrots

Alternative entrée

Paupiettes de Veau Citronnées
(Rolled Escalopes of Veal with Lemon)

6–8 (about 1½ lb) veal escalopes
2 tablespoons butter
1 onion, chopped
1 cup white wine
peeled rind of 1 lemon
1 cup well-flavored chicken or veal stock
kneaded butter (made with 2 tablespoons butter and 1 tablespoon flour)

For stuffing
1 large onion, finely chopped
¼ cup butter
1 cup (½ lb) finely chopped cooked ham
6 tablespoons fresh white breadcrumbs
1 tablespoon chopped parsley
½ teaspoon thyme
salt and pepper
1 egg, beaten to mix

Method
Pound the veal escalopes to make them as thin as possible.

To make the stuffing: cook onion in butter until soft but not browned. Take from heat and stir in the ham, breadcrumbs, herbs and seasoning to taste. Stir in the egg to bind the mixture and spread on the escalopes; roll them up neatly and tie each escalope several times with string.

In a skillet or shallow flameproof casserole brown the escalopes on all sides in butter. Add onion, cook until soft, then add the wine, lemon rind and stock. Cover and simmer veal for 20–25 minutes or until very tender.

Remove escalopes from the pan and discard the strings. Simmer the gravy until it is well reduced, strain, bring back to a boil and thicken slightly if necessary, by adding kneaded butter a little at a time and stirring until thickened; taste gravy for seasoning.

Serve the paupiettes on a bed of mashed potatoes with the gravy spooned over top. Garnish the platter with baby carrots sprinkled with chopped parsley. If you like, serve tomato and orange salad separately.

To flatten escalopes, lay them between 2 sheets of wax paper and pound them with a cutlet bat to ¼ inch thickness.

Accompaniments to alternative entrée

Tomato and Orange Salad

2 tomatoes, peeled and thinly sliced
3 oranges
1 teaspoon sugar
¼ cup vinaigrette dressing (see page 93)

Method
Sprinkle the sugar over the tomatoes. Thinly peel the rind from 1 orange, cut the strips into needle-like shreds, blanch in boiling water for 1 minute and drain. Cut the remaining rind and pith from the oranges with a serrated-edge knife and section them, discarding the membrane, or slice them.

Arrange the oranges in a serving dish with the tomatoes, spoon over the vinaigrette dressing and scatter the shredded peel on top.

Vichy (Glazed) Carrots

For 4 people: in a saucepan put 1–1½ lb carrots, trimmed, peeled and left whole if young, or quartered if large. Add ½ teaspoon salt, 1 teaspoon sugar, 2 tablespoons butter and water barely to cover. Cover and cook until the carrots are tender, remove the lid and boil until the water has completely evaporated, leaving a sticky glaze. Sprinkle with 1 tablespoon finely chopped mint or parsley.

Luscious hazelnut meringue cake is filled with raspberries and Chantilly cream

Dessert

Hazelnut Meringue Cake
with Melba Sauce

4 egg whites
1 cup sugar
1 teaspoon vanilla
½ teaspoon vinegar
1 cup shelled hazelnuts,
  browned and finely ground
2 cups Chantilly cream
1 pint fresh red raspberries
  or 1 package frozen red
  raspberries (thawed and
  drained)
confectioners' sugar (for
  sprinkling)

2 cups Melba sauce (to serve —
see page 124)

*Two 8 inch cake pans; pastry
bag and a medium star tube*

Method
Line the pans with a circle of wax paper, grease them and sprinkle with flour, discarding the excess. Set oven at moderately hot (375°F).

Beat the egg whites until they hold a stiff peak. Add the sugar 1 tablespoon at a time and continue beating until the mixture is very stiff and stands in peaks. Beat in the vanilla and vinegar and fold in the ground hazelnuts.

Divide the mixture between the 2 prepared pans and smooth the tops. Bake in heated oven for 30–40 minutes. The top of the meringue will be crisp and the inside soft like marshmallow (due to addition of the vinegar). Turn meringue cake out onto wire racks to cool.

Spread two-thirds of the Chantilly cream on one layer of the meringue. Pile raspberries on top and replace the other layer. Sprinkle the top with confectioners' sugar. Spoon the remaining cream into the pastry bag fitted with the star tube and pipe rosettes on top of the cake to decorate. **Watchpoint:** layer the meringue with filling at least 3 hours before serving so the cake softens and can be cut into neat wedges without crumbling.

Serve the Melba sauce separately.

Chantilly Cream

For 2 cups: whip 1 cup heavy cream until it starts to thicken; add 1 tablespoon sugar and ½ teaspoon vanilla; continue whipping until the cream holds a shape. (If the kitchen is hot or the sugar and vanilla are added before the first whipping, the cream will not thicken; in very hot weather chill the cream, bowl and beater before whipping.)

To brown hazelnuts: bake them in a moderately hot oven (375°F) for 8–10 minutes. Then rub them briskly in a rough cloth to remove the dry skins. Grind the nuts in a rotary cheese grater or work them a few at a time in a blender.

To make Chantilly cream, whip the cream until it starts to thicken, then add the sugar and vanilla and continue whipping until the cream holds a shape

Spoon two-thirds of the Chantilly cream onto one layer of the meringue cake

MENUS FOR THE WEEKEND

The key to carefree weekend entertaining is good planning. Decide on your menus and do the shopping early so you can spend some time later in the week preparing ahead and making dishes like veal parisienne and French fruit braid, that need only a last-minute attention.

You can coordinate different dishes to save both time and money. For example, poach a roasting chicken or fowl on Thursday or Friday, take the meat from the bones and store it in the refrigerator to use for chicken pilaf for Saturday lunch. The bones make good stock for veal parisienne and the liver will help to make chicken liver pâté for an appetizer.

If you have a freezer you can start preparing a month ahead if you want to, so that besides dishes intended for a particular menu you will have an ample supply of snacks and rolls that can be baked at a moment's notice. If you don't use them at once, they will keep for another occasion.

FRIDAY DINNER

★ Consommé with Mushrooms

★ Beef Roll or
★ Veal Parisienne
Potato Salad
★ Tomato Salad
Green Salad

★ Gâteau Belle Hélène

Consommé with Mushrooms

Finely slice 2 fresh mushrooms. Heat 2 cans consommé, add 3 tablespoons sherry and pour into bowls. Float a few mushroom slices on consommé in each bowl and sprinkle with chopped chives.

Veal Parisienne

1½ lb lean veal, cut into cubes
2 hard-cooked eggs, sliced
1 tablespoon chopped parsley
½ lb piece of bacon
salt and pepper
2½ cups chicken stock
½ envelope gelatin

For garnish
leaves of Boston lettuce
bunch of watercress

Charlotte mold or deep pan
(2 quart capacity)

Method

Decorate the bottom of the mold or pan with sliced egg and sprinkle with parsley.

Blanch the bacon and grind it. Chop any leftover hard-cooked egg and add to the veal with the bacon. Season and mix well with 1½ cups chicken stock.

Spoon this mixture carefully into the mold or pan, cover with foil and bake in a moderately hot oven (325°F)

for 1½–2 hours or until firm to the touch.

In a small pan sprinkle the gelatin over the remaining stock, let stand 5 minutes until spongy; dissolve over gentle heat. Season it well and spoon carefully down the sides of the mold or pan. Chill at least 4 hours until very firm; the mold can be kept, covered, for 2–3 days in the refrigerator.

Just before serving, dip the mold or pan quickly into warm water, turn out onto a platter and garnish with lettuce leaves and watercress. Serve with potato salad and tomato salad.

Spoon the veal, bacon and chicken stock mixture into the mold on top of the sliced egg and chopped parsley

Tomato Salad

4–5 ripe tomatoes, peeled and sliced
1 teaspoon sugar
2 shallots or scallions finely chopped
1 clove of garlic, crushed (optional)
1 tablespoon chopped parsley
1 teaspoon oregano or basil
½ cup vinaigrette dressing (see box)

Method

Arrange the tomato slices, overlapping, in a dish and sprinkle them with sugar. Add the shallots or scallions, garlic, if used, and herbs to the vinaigrette dressing and spoon over the tomatoes.

Cover the salad and leave (but do not chill) for 1–2 hours for the flavors to blend.

Vinaigrette Dressing

For ½ cup: mix 2 tablespoons cider, tarragon or red or white wine vinegar with ½ teaspoon salt and ½ teaspoon freshly ground black pepper. Gradually add 6 tablespoons olive or peanut oil, whisking until the dressing thickens slightly. Taste for seasoning. Chopped fresh herbs (thyme, marjoram, basil or parsley) are an excellent addition, as is a pinch of sugar.

TIMETABLE

Friday Dinner

Consommé with mushrooms: make and heat just before serving.

Veal parisienne: prepare 2–3 days before; keep covered in refrigerator. Turn out and garnish just before serving.

Beef roll: if using mock glaze, prepare day before. Make and cook beef roll day before; store in refrigerator. Trim ends of roll and garnish just before serving.

Potato salad: cook potatoes and mix with dressing in morning. Add mayonnaise 1–2 hours before serving.

Tomato salad: prepare in the morning. Cover but do not refrigerate.

Green salad: make dressing day before. Wash greens in morning and store in plastic bag in refrigerator. Toss just before serving.

Gâteau belle Hélène: bake 1–2 days before and store in airtight container. Decorate 1–2 hours before serving.

Note: dishes starred in the menus on pages 93–99 are given in this Volume; for others refer to the Index. Quantities are enough for 4 people unless otherwise stated.

Veal parisienne mold is garnished with lettuce and watercress

Gâteau Belle Hélène

2 squares (2 oz) unsweetened
   chocolate, cut up
$\frac{1}{2}$ cup water
3 eggs
$\frac{1}{2}$ cup sugar
$\frac{1}{2}$ cup flour

To decorate
2 dessert pears
1$\frac{1}{2}$ cups Chantilly cream
   (made with $\frac{3}{4}$ cup heavy
   cream, 2–3 teaspoons sugar
   and $\frac{1}{2}$ teaspoon vanilla
   extract)
confectioners' sugar (for
   sprinkling)

*8 inch springform pan; pastry
bag and star tube*

Method
Grease and flour the cake pan.
Set the oven at moderate
(350°F).

Melt the chocolate in water
over gentle heat, stirring until
thick and creamy. Cool to
tepid.

Beat the eggs and sugar
with a rotary beater over a pan
of hot water for 5–6 minutes
or until the mixture leaves a
ribbon trail when beater is
lifted. Remove from the heat
and beat until cool. If using an
electric mixer, no heat is
necessary. Stir in the chocolate mixture.

Sift the flour and fold it
into the egg mixture in 2–3
portions. Pour the batter into
the prepared pan and bake in
heated oven for 30 minutes
or until the cake springs back
when lightly pressed with a
fingertip. Cool the cake for 5
minutes in the pan, then turn
it out onto a wire rack to cool
completely. Store 1–2 days in
an airtight container, if you
like.

To decorate: pare, core and
slice the pears. Split the cake
and sandwich it with Chantilly

Beef Roll

2 lb lean ground beef
$\frac{1}{2}$ lb ground salt pork
4 cups fresh white breadcrumbs
1 onion, finely chopped
1 teaspoon mixed herbs
   (thyme, basil, oregano)
salt and pepper
3–4 eggs, beaten to mix
2–3 thick slices of onion

To finish
mock glaze, or 2 tablespoons
   browned breadcrumbs
bunch of watercress
1–2 tomatoes, peeled and
   sliced

Method
Mix the salt pork with the beef,
breadcrumbs and chopped
onion. Add the herbs and
plenty of seasoning and stir in

enough egg to bind the mixture.

On a wet board shape the
mixture into a roll 8–9 inches
long and wrap in foil, folding
the seams securely and
pleating them to allow for
expansion during cooking.

Put the onion slices in a
pan, lay the roll on top, cover
with boiling water and lid and
simmer 1$\frac{1}{2}$ hours or until the
roll is firm. (The slices of
onion are used only to keep
the roll off the bottom of the
pan and the foil wrapping
prevents any transfer of
flavors to the beef.)

Lift out the beef roll, cool it
slightly, then press it lightly
between 2 plates until cold.
The roll can be kept 1–2
days in the refrigerator.

A short time before serving,
remove the foil and brush the

meat with mock glaze or
sprinkle the roll with browned
breadcrumbs. Trim a slice
from each end to neaten,
arrange the beef roll on a
platter and garnish with watercress and tomato slices. Serve
with potato salad and green
salad.

Mock Glaze

Sprinkle 1 envelope gela-
tin over $\frac{1}{2}$ can consommé
in a small pan. Leave 5
minutes until spongy,
then dissolve over a pan
of hot water. Stir in the
remaining $\frac{1}{2}$ can consommé. Use the glaze
when cool and on the
point of setting.

cream and pear slices, reserving some cream. Replace the top and sprinkle with confectioners' sugar. Put the remaining cream into the pastry bag fitted with the star tube and pipe rosettes of cream on top of the cake.

SATURDAY LUNCH

★ *Seafood Pilaf or*
★ *Chicken Pilaf*
Green Salad

Fresh Fruit
★ *Orange Raisin Cake*

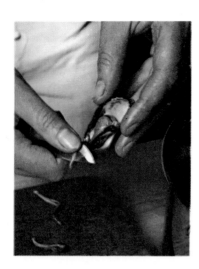

For seafood pilaf, remove cooked mussels from their shells and pull off the beards; discard any mussels that do not open

TIMETABLE

Saturday Lunch

Seafood pilaf: prepare the pilaf the day before, cover and refrigerate. Reheat in a moderate oven (350°F) for 15–20 minutes or until very hot. Prepare seafood in morning and add to pilaf just before serving.

Chicken pilaf: make pilaf the day before. Cook the bird and cut into strips the day before. To serve, combine chicken and mushrooms, cheese and rice and reheat dish in a moderate oven (350°F) for 15–20 minutes or until very hot.

Green salad: make the vinaigrette dressing the day before. Wash salad greens in the morning and store in plastic bag in refrigerator. Toss just before serving.

Orange raisin cake: prepare up to 1 week before; store in an airtight container.

Note: dishes starred in the menus on pages 93–99 are given in this Volume; for others refer to the Index. Quantities are enough for 4 people unless otherwise stated.

Seafood Pilaf

2 quarts fresh mussels or
  2 cans (9 oz each) cooked
  mussels
1 cup white wine
1 cup water
bouquet garni (1 bay leaf,
  1 stalk of celery, 3–4 stalks
  of parsley)
6 peppercorns
4–6 ($\frac{1}{2}$ lb) uncooked jumbo
  shrimps or rock lobster tails
dash of Tabasco
2 cups ($\frac{1}{2}$ lb) mushrooms,
  trimmed
$\frac{1}{4}$ cup butter
$\frac{1}{2}$ lb medium peeled and
  uncooked shrimps
pinch of ground mace

For pilaf
1$\frac{1}{4}$ cups rice
$\frac{1}{4}$ cup butter
1 medium onion, finely sliced
about 1 cup chicken stock
salt and pepper

Method

To prepare fresh mussels: wash them well, scrubbing to remove any weed; discard any mussels with open shells that do not close when tapped.

Place the mussels in a kettle with the wine, water, bouquet garni and peppercorns. Cover, bring slowly to a boil and cook, shaking the pan occasionally, for 5 minutes or until the mussels are opened. Remove mussels from the shells, discarding the beards and any that do not open, and reserve.

Strain the cooking liquid through a double thickness of cheesecloth or through a coffee filter paper.

Watchpoint: straining the liquid removes any sand.

Add the cooking liquid to the stock for the pilaf. If using canned mussels, drain them and add the liquid with wine and water to the stock.

Set the oven at moderate (350°F).

To prepare the pilaf: melt two-thirds of the butter in a flameproof casserole, add the onion and cook slowly until soft but not browned. Add rice and cook, stirring for 2–3 minutes or until the grains are transparent. Add 2$\frac{1}{2}$ cups of the mixed stock and mussel liquid, bring to a boil and taste before adding seasoning because the mussel liquid may be salty. Cover the pot and cook in heated oven for 20 minutes, adding extra stock after 15 minutes if pan is dry.

Put the jumbo shrimps or lobster tails in a pan with water to cover, add salt and a dash of Tabasco, cover the pan and simmer 4–6 minutes, depending on size, until the shrimps or lobsters are pink. Drain and peel them.

Sauté the mushrooms in 3 tablespoons of the butter for 1 minute. Add the medium shrimps with the mace and cook, stirring, until the shrimps are pink and mushrooms tender.

Add cooked jumbo shrimps or lobster tails, dot with 1 tablespoon butter, cover and keep warm.

When the pilaf is cooked, cool it slightly, then stir in the remaining butter with a fork. Add the mussels and the mushroom and seafood mixture, toss well over heat and serve.

Chicken Pilaf

4–4½ lb roasting chicken or
   fowl
1 onion, peeled
1 carrot, peeled
1 stalk of celery
bouquet garni
1 teaspoon salt
6 peppercorns
2 cups (½ lb) mushrooms,
   thickly sliced
3 tablespoons butter

For pilaf
1¼ cups rice
¼ cup butter
1 medium onion, finely chopped
2½–3 cups chicken stock (from
   cooking chicken)
pinch of saffron, soaked in
   ¼ cup boiling water for
   30 minutes
black pepper, freshly ground
1 bay leaf
3 tablespoons grated Parmesan
   cheese

Method

Put the bird in a kettle with the vegetables, bouquet garni, salt and peppercorns and water to cover. Cover pan, bring to a boil and simmer 1–1½ hours or until the bird is tender. Cool in the liquid, then remove the bird, strain and measure the stock.

Set the oven at moderate (350°F).

To make the pilaf: melt 3 tablespoons butter in a flame-proof casserole, add the onion and cook slowly until soft. Stir in the rice and cook 2–3 minutes or until the grains are transparent. Add 2½ cups of the chicken stock with saffron liquid and a little pepper. Bring to a boil, put bay leaf on top, cover and bake in heated oven for 20 minutes. Add more stock after 15 minutes if the pan is dry.

Cut chicken meat into strips, discarding bones and skin. Sauté mushrooms for 1–2

minutes in butter until tender.

When rice is cooked, remove bay leaf, dot rice with remaining butter, sprinkle with cheese and leave 3–5 minutes. Add the chicken and mushrooms, stir with 2 forks over heat until mixed and serve.

Orange Raisin Cake

grated rind of 1 orange
¼ cup orange juice
2 cups raisins
3 cups self-rising flour
¼ teaspoon salt
½ teaspoon grated nutmeg
¾ cup butter
¾ cup dark brown sugar
3 eggs

Large loaf pan (9 X 5 X 3 inches)

Method

Grease the loaf pan and line the base with wax paper. Set the oven at moderate (350°F).

Sift the flour with the salt and nutmeg into a bowl, add the butter and rub in with the fingertips until the mixture resembles crumbs. Stir in the sugar, raisins and orange rind and make a well in the center.

Beat the eggs with the orange juice until frothy. Pour into the flour mixture and stir until smooth. Spoon the mixture into the prepared pan and bake in heated oven for 1–1¼ hours or until a toothpick or skewer inserted in the center comes out clean.

Cool the cake in the pan for 30 minutes, then turn out onto a wire rack to cool completely. Store for up to 1 week in an airtight container.

SATURDAY DINNER

★ *Smoked Salmon Rolls with Shrimps*

★ *Fillet of Beef Italienne*
★ *Gnocchi Romana Green Beans*
or
★ *Paupiettes de Veau Citronnées Baby Carrots Mashed Potatoes*
or
Tomato & Orange Salad
★ *Hazelnut Meringue Cake with Melba Sauce*

(see menu, pages 84–91)

Saturday dinner recipes serve 6 people, allowing for 2 extra guests (see pages 84–91). All the other recipes serve 4 people.

Note: dishes starred in the menus on pages 96–99 are given in this Volume; for others refer to the Index. Quantities are enough for 4 people unless otherwise stated.

SATURDAY BRUNCH

★ *Scottish Poached Eggs Crisp Bacon*
★ *Honey Twist*
★ *French Fruit Braid*
Coffee or Tea

TIMETABLE

Sunday Brunch

Scottish poached eggs: cook and flake Finnan haddie, prepare mornay sauce and croûtes day before and keep covered separately in refrigerator.

To serve: sauté the mushrooms and add fish; poach eggs and reheat croûtes in moderate oven (350°F) for 4–5 minutes. Drain eggs, set on croûtes with fish and mushroom mixture on top. Reheat sauce in a saucepan, spoon over fish and brown under broiler. Broil bacon.

French fruit braid: make the dough, knead and let rise twice; add filling, shape, cover tightly and refrigerate 1–2 days before. To serve: let rise (if necessary) and bake.

Honey twist: make the dough, knead and let rise twice; shape, add topping, cover tightly and refrigerate 1–2 days before. To serve: let rise (if necessary) and bake.

Serve French fruit braid (front) and honey twist (back) for a tempting brunch

Scottish Poached Eggs

8 eggs
1 lb Finnan haddie
1 cup ($\frac{1}{4}$ lb) mushrooms, sliced
little milk
8 slices of bread (for croûtes)
$\frac{1}{4}$ cup oil and butter, mixed (for croûtes)
mornay sauce (made with
   3 tablespoons butter,
   2 tablespoons flour,
   1$\frac{1}{2}$ cups milk, 2 egg yolks,
   2 tablespoons grated
   Parmesan cheese)
salt and pepper
2 tablespoons butter

Method
Poach the eggs and keep in a bowl of warm water while preparing the remaining ingredients.

Trim the Finnan haddie, put in a shallow pan or skillet, cover with cold water and a little milk and bring slowly to a boil. Take from the heat, cover the pan and let stand 10 minutes. The fish should flake easily; if it does not, simmer 5 minutes longer. Drain the fish, remove the skin and bones and flake the flesh with a fork. Keep warm.

To make the croûtes: cut large circles from the bread and fry them in oil and butter until brown on both sides. Drain the croûtes and keep warm.

Make the mornay sauce, adding the egg yolks with the cheese, and season to taste.

Arrange the croûtes in a baking dish.

In a frying pan melt the 2 tablespoons butter, sauté the mushrooms, stirring, over high heat for 1 minute. Season, add the Finnan haddie and heat well.

Drain the eggs on paper towels, set on the croûtes and spread the fish and mushroom mixture on top. Spoon over the mornay sauce, brown lightly under the broiler and serve with crisp bacon.

Basic Dough for Coffeecake

4 cups flour
$\frac{1}{2}$ teaspoon salt
1 cup milk
$\frac{1}{2}$ cup butter
1 package dry or 1 cake compressed yeast
$\frac{1}{2}$ cup sugar
2 eggs, beaten to mix

Method
Sift the flour with the salt into a bowl. Warm the milk with the butter until melted, then cool to lukewarm. Sprinkle or crumble the yeast on top and leave 5 minutes or until dissolved. Stir in the sugar and eggs.

Make a well in the flour, add yeast mixture and stir to form a smooth dough. Work with your hand until the dough pulls away from the sides of the bowl, then turn out onto a floured board and knead 5 minutes or until the dough is smooth and elastic.

Place the dough in a warm greased bowl, turn so it is lightly greased all over, cover with a damp cloth and let rise in a warm place for $\frac{3}{4}$–1 hour or until it is doubled in bulk.

Knead the dough lightly to knock out the air, pull the sides to the center, turn it over, cover and let rise again for 30 minutes before shaping and baking.

French Fruit Braid

4 cup quantity of basic coffee-cake dough

For filling
3 medium tart apples, pared, cored and chopped
1$\frac{1}{4}$ cups raisins
$\frac{1}{2}$ cup dark brown sugar
$\frac{1}{2}$ teaspoon ground cinnamon
2 tablespoons butter

For icing
$\frac{1}{2}$ cup confectioners' sugar, sifted
1–1$\frac{1}{2}$ tablespoons water

Method
Grease a baking sheet.

To prepare the filling: put all the ingredients in a pan, cover and cook over low heat, stirring occasionally, until the apple is soft and pulpy. Let cool.

On a floured board or the prepared baking sheet, roll or pat out the dough to an 8 X 14 inch rectangle.

Spread the fruit mixture down the center of the dough rectangle in a 3 inch strip. At each side of the filling make diagonal cuts 2 inches long at 1 inch intervals. Fold the dough over at the end and cross strips from each side to form a braid. Tuck the last 2 strips under the end of the braid.

Cover the braid with a damp cloth and let rise in a warm place for 20–30 minutes or until doubled in bulk.

Set oven at hot (400°F). Bake the braid for 30–35 minutes or until brown.

To make the icing: stir enough water into the confectioners' sugar to form a smooth thin paste. Brush over the braid while still warm.

For French fruit braid cut the dough diagonally on each side of the filling to form strips

Fold over the dough at the end and cross the strips over the filling to give a braided effect

Honey Twist

4 cup quantity of basic coffee-
    cake dough

For topping
$\frac{1}{4}$ cup butter, melted
6 tablespoons clear honey
$\frac{1}{4}$ cup sugar
$\frac{1}{4}$ cup flour
$\frac{1}{2}$ cup chopped almonds

10 inch round cake pan

Method
Thoroughly grease cake pan.

On a floured board, shape the dough into a long narrow roll about 1 inch thick. Coil the roll into the prepared pan, starting at the outside and twisting as well as turning; leave a little space between the coils. Cover the dough with a damp cloth and let rise in a warm place for 35—40 minutes or until well risen.

Set oven at hot (400°F).

Mix all the ingredients for the topping and spoon over the dough. Bake in heated oven for 30—35 minutes or until the bread is browned. Slice and serve warm with butter.

SUNDAY SUPPER

Broiled or Pan fried Steak or Hamburgers

★ *Potato Goulash*

★ *Grapefruit Parfait*

TIMETABLE

Sunday Supper

Steak or hamburgers: broil or pan fry just before serving.

Potato goulash: prepare 1—2 days before, but do not complete cooking. Cover and refrigerate. Just before serving bake in moderate oven (350°F) for 15—18 minutes or until the potatoes are tender. Spoon over the yogurt or cream and serve.

Grapefruit parfait: prepare up to 2 weeks before, put in ice cube trays, cover and freeze.

Note: dishes starred in the menus on pages 93—99 are given in this Volume; for others refer to the Index. Quantities are enough for 4 people unless otherwise stated.

Potato Goulash

12—14 small new potatoes or
    3—4 large potatoes
1 tablespoon oil
2 medium onions, finely
    chopped
small clove of garlic, crushed
    (optional)
2 teaspoons paprika
2 teaspoons flour
1 cup stock or water
2 tablespoons wine vinegar
salt and pepper
$\frac{1}{2}$ teaspoon caraway seeds
    (optional)
1 green pepper, cored, seeded,
    cut into strips and blanched
2 tomatoes, peeled, seeded and
    cut into strips
$\frac{1}{4}$ cup plain yogurt, sour cream
    or heavy cream

Method
Scrub or peel the small new potatoes or peel large potatoes, cut in quarters and trim the sharp edges. Cook potatoes in boiling salted water for 10—12 minutes or until almost tender.

In a flameproof casserole heat the oil, add the onions and garlic, if used, and cook until golden brown. Stir in the paprika and cook over low heat for 1 minute. Take from heat, stir in the flour and pour on the stock or water and vinegar. Season and bring to a boil.

Drain the potatoes and add to the casserole with the caraway seeds, if used, the green pepper and tomatoes. Season to taste, cover and bake in a moderate oven (350°F) for 5—10 minutes until very hot.

Spoon over the yogurt or cream, shake the pot gently to blend and serve hot.

Grapefruit Parfait

juice of 2 grapefruits
finely grated rind of
    1 grapefruit
2 tablespoons thick honey
1 cup heavy cream, whipped
    until it holds a soft shape
2 egg whites
3 tablespoons sugar
8—12 ladyfingers (for serving)

4 coupe or parfait glasses

Method
Mix the grapefruit juice and rind with the honey. Beat into the cream and continue beating until the mixture holds a stiff peak.

Beat the egg whites until they hold a stiff peak and beat in the sugar until the mixture is glossy. Fold the egg whites into the grapefruit mixture and pour into an ice cube tray. Freeze for about 2 hours.

Take the parfait from the tray, mix well and freeze again for 4 hours. Mix again, return to the tray and cover with wax paper. You may freeze the parfait for up to 2 weeks if necessary.

To serve, pile the parfait in coupe glasses and pass ladyfingers separately.

HOW TO MAKE CREPES (1)

The wafer-thin French pancakes called crêpes are remarkably versatile; they can be layered or filled with a variety of sweet and savory mixtures or served with lemon hard sauce or a fruit sauce; crêpes are easy, inexpensive and can be made in large quantities. An experienced crêpe cook can make them twice as quickly by keeping two or even three pans going at once. Crêpes can be layered with wax paper and stored in the refrigerator for several days, and plain or filled they freeze well so they are ideal for entertaining.

Points to remember

1 To avoid lumps when making the crêpe batter, stir in the milk gradually.

2 Let the batter stand for at least 30 minutes before using so that grains of starch in the flour can soften in the milk.

3 The batter will thicken on standing and more milk may be needed; it should be the consistency of light cream.

4 To cook the crêpes, wipe out the pan and set it over moderate heat. When very hot, add a few drops of oil. A good crêpe should be wafer-thin with a crisp, lacy edge. Butter or oil in the batter gives this effect, so little or no fat is needed in the pan.

5 Pour 2–3 tablespoons of batter into the pan and immediately roll it around clockwise to coat base of pan evenly (2–3 tablespoons batter is enough for a 6 inch pan).

6 Cook until the bottom of the crêpe is golden brown. Run a thin metal spatula under the edges to loosen the crêpe, then raise it slightly with the fingers and slip the knife underneath. Turn the crêpe over and cook for about 10 seconds or until brown on the other side. Alternatively toss the crêpe over. Turn it out on a rack or paper towel.

7 Continue to cook the crêpes, stacking them one on top of another, until you have as many as you need. Leftover batter can be stored, covered, in refrigerator up to 3 days.

8 If not using crêpes immediately, cover the stack with a bowl or a cloth to keep warm.

9 To store the crêpes, place a sheet of wax paper between each one, wrap them in foil or a plastic bag and refrigerate for up to 4 days or wrap the same way and freeze.

10 To reheat crêpes: brush a baking sheet or heatproof dish with 2 tablespoons melted butter. Peel off the crêpes and lay them, overlapping, on the sheet. Brush them with more melted butter to exclude air and protect them while heating, and bake in a hot oven (400°F) for 3–4 minutes.

11 If crêpes are to be stuffed, fill them before storing in the refrigerator or freezer and bake them with the stuffing inside in a hot oven (400°F) for 8–15 minutes or until hot.

Crêpe Pan
The right pan is very important for making crêpes. It should be small, with a base about 6 inches in diameter, and made of cast iron or heavy aluminum. True crêpe pans are shallow (the sides are about $\frac{3}{4}$ inch high) to make tossing easy and they are available in specialty kitchen stores. You can also use an omelet pan, which has a curved edge and taller sides, or a small skillet, but choose a very shallow one.

Ideally the pan should be kept for making crêpes and omelets only, so it is never washed. To clean it: wipe it well with a damp cloth or a paper towel dipped in salt, then rub it lightly with a few drops of oil; this helps prevent sticking and stops cast iron from rusting.

Basic Crêpe Batter

$1\frac{1}{2}$ cups milk
1 cup flour
pinch of salt
1 egg
1 egg yolk
1 tablespoon melted butter or oil

Makes about 18 crêpes.

Method
Sift the flour with the salt into a bowl, make a well in the center and add the egg and egg yolk. Pour in the milk slowly, stirring constantly and, when half is added, stir in the melted butter or oil. Beat well until smooth.

Add the remaining milk, cover and let stand at room temperature for at least 30 minutes before using. The batter should be the consistency of light cream — if it is too thick, add a little more milk.

Quantity Terms
Terms like $1\frac{1}{2}$ cup quantity of crêpe batter refer to batter made with $1\frac{1}{2}$ cups milk, with other ingredients in proportion as given above.

Pour the milk slowly into the flour and egg mixture, stirring

Make a well in the flour and add one egg and an egg yolk

Tilt pan so that the batter spreads evenly over bottom

SAVORY CREPES

The following savory crêpe recipes will serve 4 people as a light entrée or 6 as an appetizer.

Spinach Crêpes

1½ cup quantity of basic crêpe batter
2 tablespoons melted butter
2 tablespoons grated Parmesan cheese

For filling
1 lb fresh spinach, stems removed
3 tablespoons butter
1 shallot, finely chopped
2 teaspoons tomato paste
3 tomatoes, peeled, seeded and coarsely chopped
1 teaspoon paprika
4 hard-cooked eggs, sliced
salt
black pepper, freshly ground

Makes about 18 crêpes.

Method
Prepare the crêpe batter, cover and let stand for at least 30 minutes.

Cook the spinach in boiling salted water for 5 minutes or until tender and drain thoroughly, pressing out the water with a plate or spoon.

Melt 2 tablespoons of the butter and cook the shallot over gentle heat until soft but not browned. Stir in tomato paste, tomatoes and paprika and simmer 2–3 minutes, stirring. Add the hard-cooked eggs, season and keep warm.

Fry the crêpes and pile on a warm plate.

Melt the remaining 1 tablespoon butter and toss the spinach in it until very hot. Spread a little spinach on each crêpe, add a spoonful of tomato and egg mixture and roll them up like cigars.

Arrange the crêpes in a buttered baking dish, brush with the melted butter and sprinkle with cheese. Brown lightly under the broiler and serve.

Chicken Crêpes with Curry

1½ cup quantity of basic crêpe batter

For curry sauce
2 cups milk
bouquet garni
6 peppercorns
3 tablespoons butter
1 onion, diced
1 carrot, diced
1 stalk of celery, diced
1 tablespoon curry powder
2 tablespoons flour
salt and pepper
¼ cup heavy cream
3 tablespoons grated Parmesan cheese (to finish)

For filling
1½ cups cooked chicken, cut in strips
2 hard-cooked eggs, chopped

Makes about 18 crêpes.

Method
Prepare the crêpe batter, cover and let stand at least 30 minutes.

To make the curry sauce: scald the milk in a pan with bouquet garni and peppercorns, cover and let infuse for 5 minutes; strain.

Melt half the butter in a saucepan, add the onion, carrot and celery and cook slowly until soft but not browned. Add the remaining butter with the curry powder and cook 2–3 minutes longer. Blend in the flour and infused milk, add salt to taste and stir the sauce until boiling. Simmer it for about 10 minutes, then strain.

To make the filling: mix about two-thirds of the sauce with the chicken and eggs, season the mixture and keep it warm.

Fry the crêpes and stack them on a warm dish.

Put a tablespoon of filling in the center of each crêpe, fold in half, then one side over the other, and arrange in a buttered baking dish.

Add the cream to the remaining curry sauce and spoon over the crêpes to coat them. Sprinkle cheese on top of the crêpes and bake in a hot oven (400°F) for 7–8 minutes or until brown and crisp.

Ham Crêpes

1½ cup quantity of basic crêpe batter
3 tablespoons grated Parmesan cheese (to finish)

For filling
12 thin slices of cooked ham
½ cup butter
2 shallots, finely chopped
3 cups (¾ lb) mushrooms, finely chopped
2 teaspoons flour
½ cup stock or light cream
salt and pepper
1 tablespoon chopped parsley
1 teaspoon thyme

Makes about 18 crêpes.

Method
Prepare the crêpe batter, cover and let stand for 30 minutes.

To make the filling: melt ¼ cup butter in a frying pan, add the shallots and cook until soft but not browned. Add the mushrooms and continue cooking over moderately high heat until all the moisture has evaporated, stirring occasionally. Blend in the flour and stock or cream, season and cook the mixture, stirring, for 2 minutes. Take from heat and add the herbs.

Fry the crêpes. Place a slice of ham and a large spoonful of mushroom filling on each one and fold in half, then one side over the other and arrange in a buttered baking dish.

Melt the remaining butter and brush or pour over the crêpes. Sprinkle the crêpes with cheese and bake in a hot oven (400°F) for 7–10 minutes or until very hot.

For ham crêpes, put a large spoonful of filling on the ham, fold the filled crêpe in half, then fold one side over the other and bake

Crêpes Beatrix

For batter
1 cup flour
pinch of salt
2 eggs
1½ cups milk
¼ cup finely grated Gouda or
  dry Cheddar cheese
2 tablespoons melted butter
  or oil

For filling
2–3 smoked trout or any
  smoked white fish
béchamel sauce, made with
  3 tablespoons butter,
  3 tablespoons flour and
  1¾ cups milk (infused with
  6 peppercorns, slice of onion,
  blade of mace, ½ bay leaf)
1 tablespoon prepared
  horseradish
2 tablespoons heavy cream
salt and pepper

To finish
¼ cup heavy cream
2 tablespoons grated
  Parmesan cheese

Makes 18–20 crêpes.

Method
Prepare the crêpe batter (see page 102), adding the grated cheese after half the milk has been added. Cover and let stand for at least 30 minutes.

Remove the skin and bones from the trout or white fish and divide the fillets into 18–20 neat pieces.

Make the béchamel sauce, add prepared horseradish and 2 tablespoons heavy cream and season to taste. Fry crêpes and stack on a warm dish.

Fill each one with a piece of fish fillet and a spoonful of sauce, roll up like a cigar and arrange in a buttered baking dish. Spoon the cream over the crêpes, sprinkle with Parmesan cheese and bake in a moderately hot oven (375°F) for 10 minutes or until hot.

SWEET CREPES

The following sweet crêpe recipes will serve 4 people.

Crêpes Sultane

For batter
1 cup flour
pinch of salt
2 eggs
1 cup milk
1 tablespoon melted butter
2 tablespoons sugar
2 tablespoons heavy cream
1 tablespoon rum (optional)
1 dry macaroon, crushed

For filling
2 bananas
4 slices of fresh or canned
  pineapple
¼ cup apricot jam

To finish
2 tablespoons confectioners'
  sugar, sifted
2 tablespoons rum

Makes about 18 crêpes.

Method
Prepare the crêpe batter (see page 102), adding the sugar and cream with the butter. Cover and let stand for at least 30 minutes. Stir in the rum, if using, and macaroon crumbs just before frying.

Cut the bananas into fairly thick diagonal slices and quarter the rings of pineapple. Stir the apricot jam into the fruit to bind it.

Fry the crêpes and stack them on a warm plate.

Spread each crêpe with a spoonful of the fruit mixture and fold – first fold both sides to the middle and then fold the whole crêpe in half.

Arrange the crêpes, overlapping, in a buttered baking dish and sprinkle with confectioners' sugar. Bake in a hot oven (425°F) for 3–5 minutes or until very hot. Heat the rum, flame it, pour it into the dish and serve the crêpes at once.

Quantity Terms
Terms like 1½ cup quantity of crêpe batter refer to batter made with 1½ cups milk, with other ingredients in proportion as given in basic crêpe recipe.

Crêpes Normande

8 cooked crêpes
3 tart apples, pared, cored
  and thinly sliced
2 tablespoons melted butter
½ cup heavy cream
½ cup sugar

Make this recipe with left-over crêpes.

Method
Lay 4 crêpes in the bottom of 4 heatproof plates or shallow baking dishes. Brush the crêpes with melted butter, lay another crêpe on each one and brush again with butter.

Set the apple slices on top and pour over the cream. Sprinkle generously with sugar and broil as far as possible from the flame for 6–8 minutes or until the sugar has caramelized and the apples are tender.

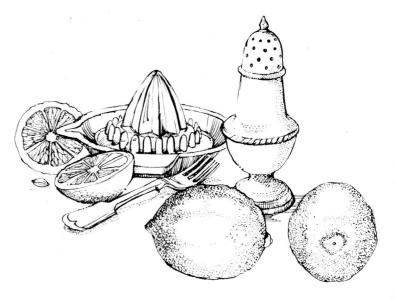

Use leftover crêpes to make crêpes normande, topped with caramelized apple slices

Apple Crêpes

1½ cup quantity of basic crêpe
    batter (see page 102), with
    1 teaspoon sugar added with
    the oil or butter

For filling
5–6 tart apples, pared, cored
    and sliced
1 tablespoon butter
¼ cup dark brown sugar
    (or to taste)
½ teaspoon ground cinnamon
grated rind of 1 lemon

For apricot jam sauce
¼ cup thick apricot jam
1 cup water
2 strips of lemon rind
1 tablespoon sugar
1–2 teaspoons arrowroot
    (mixed to a paste with 1–2
    tablespoons water) –
    optional

Makes about 18 crêpes.

Method
Prepare the crêpe batter, cover and let stand at least 30 minutes.

Spread the butter thickly in a heavy based pan, add the apples with brown sugar to taste, cinnamon and grated lemon rind. Cover and cook slowly for 10–15 minutes until tender but not too mushy.

To make the apricot jam sauce: put all ingredients except the arrowroot paste in a pan and bring slowly to a boil, stirring. Taste, and if the flavor is bland, add more jam. Simmer 5–6 minutes and strain. If the sauce is thin, add a little arrowroot paste and cook, stirring until thickened.

Fry the crêpes. Stack them on a baking dish, sandwiching them with the apple mixture. Spoon over a little apricot jam sauce to glaze the top and bake in a moderately hot oven (375°F) for about

For apple crêpes sandwich the crêpes with the apple mixture and stack in the baking dish

10 minutes or until lightly browned.

To serve, cut the crêpes into wedges, pour around more hot apricot jam sauce and serve the rest separately.

Praline Crêpes

1½ cup quantity of basic crêpe batter (see page 102)
¼ cup butter
3 tablespoons sugar
2 tablespoons praline powder (see box)
1 tablespoon rum

These crêpes go well with flamed peaches (peaches poached in syrup, drained of all but 1 tablespoon of juice, sprinkled with a little sugar heated in a chafing dish or frying pan and flamed with heated rum or brandy). Makes about 18 crêpes.

Method
Prepare the crêpe batter, cover and let stand for at least 30 minutes.

Cream the butter, gradually beat in the sugar and when the mixture is light and soft mix in the praline powder and rum.

Fry the crêpes and stack them in a warm dish.

Quickly spread each one with praline butter, roll up and arrange in a buttered baking dish. Bake in a hot oven (400°F) for 7–10 minutes until very hot and serve at once.

Praline Powder
To make about ½ cup praline powder: put ½ cup whole unblanched almonds with ½ cup sugar in a heavy based pan. Cook over low heat until the sugar melts, shaking pan occasionally. When the sugar turns a pale golden brown, stir the mixture with a metal spoon and continue cooking until it is dark brown but do not let it burn.

Pour the mixture at once onto an oiled baking sheet and leave until cold and hard. Grind it in a rotary cheese grater or a grinder or work in a blender a little at a time.

Praline powder can be stored in an airtight container — it may become soft and sticky but the flavor will not be impaired.

Quantity Terms
Terms like 1½ cup quantity of crêpe batter refer to batter made with 1½ cups milk, with other ingredients in proportion as given in basic crêpe recipe.

Crêpes à la Cévenole
(Chestnut Crêpes)

1½ cup quantity of basic crêpe batter (see page 102)
1 tablespoon sugar

For chestnut filling
1 can (8¾ oz) sweetened chestnut purée
3–4 tablespoons rum
Chantilly cream (made with 1 cup heavy cream, stiffly whipped and flavored with 1–2 tablespoons sugar and ½ teaspoon vanilla)

Makes about 18 crêpes.

Method
Prepare the crêpe batter, adding the 1 tablespoon sugar with the egg and egg yolk, cover and let stand for at least 30 minutes.

Fry the crêpes and stack them on a warm plate. Set the oven at moderately hot (375°F).

To make the filling: beat the chestnut purée with the rum, fold in half the Chantilly cream and spread a little of the mixture over each crêpe.

Roll them up like cigars and arrange them in a buttered baking dish. Cover and bake in the heated oven for 7–10 minutes or until very hot.

Spread the remaining Chantilly cream on top of the crêpes and broil them for a few moments under a very hot broiler until the cream is browned and half melted. Serve them at once.

Galetons Bretonnes
(Brittany Buckwheat Crêpes)

For batter
¾ cup buckwheat flour
pinch of salt
2 eggs
½ tablespoon olive oil
2 tablespoons brandy
1 cup buttermilk

For filling
½ cup raspberry or red currant jelly, melted
confectioners' sugar (for sprinkling)

These famous buckwheat crêpes from Brittany, France, are cooked there in flat pans called galettoires. Makes about 15 crêpes.

Method
Sift the flour into a bowl with the salt, make a well in the center and add the eggs, oil and brandy. Stir the mixture with a whisk to form a smooth batter, then beat 2–3 minutes until the batter is light. Stir in the buttermilk, cover and let stand at least 30 minutes.

Set the oven at moderately hot (375°F).

Fry the crêpes and stack them on a warm plate. Spread each one with the melted raspberry or red currant jelly.

Fold the crêpes in three, arrange them, overlapping, in a buttered baking dish and bake in the heated oven for 7–10 minutes or until very hot. Sprinkle with confectioners' sugar just before serving.

Galetons aux noisettes – buckwheat crêpes are filled with hazelnut butter

Galetons aux Noisettes
(Hazelnut Crêpes)

For batter
¾ cup buckwheat flour
pinch of salt
2 eggs
½ tablespoon olive oil
2 tablespoons brandy
1 cup buttermilk
confectioners' sugar (for
   sprinkling)

For filling
¾ cup (about ¼ lb) shelled
   hazelnuts
½ cup unsalted butter
1 cup confectioners' sugar

Makes about 15 crêpes.

Method
Prepare the batter (see method for galetons bretonnes, page 107), cover and let stand for at least 30 minutes.

Toast the hazelnuts in a moderate oven (350°F) for 12–15 minutes or until they are well browned. Let cool slightly, then rub them in a rough cloth to remove the skins. Grind hazelnuts in a rotary cheese grater or work them, a few at a time, in a blender.

To make the filling: cream the butter, beat in the confectioners' sugar and continue beating until the mixture is light and soft. Stir in the ground nuts.

Fry the crêpes and stack them on a warm plate. Spread each crêpe with hazelnut butter, fold in four and set on a greased baking sheet.

A short time before serving, heat the crêpes in a hot oven (400°F) for 5–7 minutes or until very hot. Arrange them, overlapping, on a platter, sprinkle with confectioners' sugar and serve at once.

Crêpes au Grand Marnier, filled with orange butter, are served with orange slices

Crêpes au Grand Marnier

1½ cup quantity of basic
  crêpe batter, with 1 teaspoon
  sugar added with oil or
  butter (see page 102)
¼ cup Grand Marnier or other
  orange liqueur
¼ cup orange juice
confectioners' sugar (for
  sprinkling)
orange slices (for decoration)
  —see box on page 112

For filling
½ cup unsalted butter
grated rind of 1 orange
1 cup confectioners' sugar

Makes about 18 crêpes.

Method
Prepare batter, cover and
let stand at least 30 minutes.

To make the filling: cream
the butter with the grated
orange rind, beat in the
confectioners' sugar and
continue beating until the
mixture is light and soft.

Fry the crêpes and stack
them on a warm plate. Spread
each crêpe with orange butter
roll and arrange them on a
buttered heatproof platter.

A short time before ser-
ving, in a pan heat the orange
juice and Grand Marnier or
orange liqueur until almost
boiling, pour it over the
crêpes, arrange an orange
slice on top and sprinkle with
confectioners' sugar. Bake the
crêpes in a hot oven (400°F)
for 7–10 minutes or until the
crêpes are very hot and the
sugar is caramelized. Serve
at once with the orange slices.

HOW TO MAKE PANCAKES

Pancakes are usually thought of as North American favorites but they are by no means limited to this side of the Atlantic. The Russians make their pancakes with buckwheat and call them blinis, and the Jewish tradition is to stuff them with cheese, fold them in a parcel shape and fry them as blintzes (see recipe on page 23).

The batter of traditional American pancakes is similar to that of crêpes because both are made with flour, eggs and milk, but the results are quite different. The batter for pancakes is thicker than that for crêpes, and baking powder is added so the finished pancakes are light and almost fluffy in texture. They are best eaten at once and, unlike crêpes, do not reheat well.

Points to remember

1 Pancakes are usually made with all-purpose flour, but connoisseurs maintain that buckwheat flour makes them lighter and gives more flavor (see Volume 1 for information on types of flour).

2 The batter should be mixed only until almost smooth, and it improves if made in advance and left for 1—2 hours before using.

3 Cook the pancakes in as little fat as possible; at most, the griddle or heavy skillet should only be lightly greased with oil or butter before cooking. Heat the griddle or skillet until a little water dropped on the surface bounces back. If the water stays on the surface, the griddle or skillet is too cool; if it evaporates into steam, it is too hot.

4 Pour batter from a pitcher or the tip of a spoon into even cakes. Cook until bubbles appear on the surface and the underneath is brown. Turn the pancakes over with a metal spatula and brown the other side.

5 Pile the pancakes one on top of the other, with a paper towel in between each one to absorb steam. Serve as soon as possible.

Regular Pancakes

1½ cups flour
1 teaspoon salt
3 tablespoons sugar
2 teaspoons baking powder
2 eggs, beaten to mix
3 tablespoons melted butter
1¼—1½ cups milk

Makes 24—26 pancakes (4 inch diameter).

Method

Sift the flour with the salt, sugar and baking powder into a bowl. Make a well in the center and add the eggs, melted butter and milk. Stir until the batter is almost smooth and let stand at least 1—2 hours before cooking as described at left.

Pfannkuchen

4 eggs
½ cup milk
½ cup flour
2 teaspoons sugar
pinch of salt
½ cup butter

These German pancakes are fried in butter instead of adding melted butter to the batter. Makes 4—5 pfannkuchen (7½—8 inch diameter).

Method

Beat the eggs until frothy, add the milk and continue beating until thoroughly mixed. Sift the flour with the sugar and salt and beat it, a little at a time, into the milk and egg mixture. Cover and let stand for 1 hour.

In a 7½—8 inch skillet, melt 2 tablespoons butter and, when foaming, pour in just enough batter to cover the bottom of the pan. Cook over medium heat until bubbles show on the pancake and the underneath is brown; turn and brown the other side. Set the pancake on a platter and keep warm while frying the rest of the mixture in the remaining butter.

Sprinkle the pancakes with cinnamon and sugar or pour over a little liqueur and serve with fresh or dried fruit compote and sour cream.

Dried Fruit Compote

Soak 1 lb (3 cups) mixed dried fruits in water, if necessary, according to package directions. Drain and measure 3 cups liquid. Put it in a pan with 1 cup sugar, heat until dissolved and add a piece of cinnamon stick with the rind of 1 lemon (tied in a cheesecloth bag) and its juice, 2 tablespoons kirsch, if you like, and fruit.

Bring to a boil and simmer, uncovered, for 10 minutes or until the fruit is tender. Remove the cheesecloth bag and serve the fruit compote hot.

Nockerln

5 egg yolks
2 tablespoons flour
½ teaspoon vanilla
6 egg whites
¼ cup sugar
2 tablespoons butter
Melba or other fruit sauce or confectioners' sugar (for serving) – optional

These fluffy Austrian pancakes are a cross between regular pancakes and a small soufflé omelet. Makes 8—9 nockerln.

Method

Set oven at moderate (350°F).

Beat the egg yolks for 1 minute or until thickened slightly and beat in the flour and vanilla. Whip the egg whites until they hold a stiff peak and beat in the sugar until the mixture is glossy. Stir a little of the egg white into the egg yolk mixture, then fold in the remaining egg whites as lightly as possible.

In a large skillet or flame-proof dish melt the butter and add the egg mixture in 8—9 large mounded spoonsful. Cook over medium heat for 30 seconds or until the underneath of the nockerln are golden brown.

Bake the nockerln in heated oven for 5—7 minutes or until they are browned all over. Sprinkle them generously with confectioners' sugar or serve with a Melba or fruit sauce (see page 124). Serve at once.

Buckwheat Pancakes

1½ cups buckwheat flour
½ cup all-purpose flour
½ teaspoon baking powder
½ teaspoon salt
1 teaspoon baking soda
2 teaspoons molasses, or sugar (optional)
3 cups buttermilk
2 tablespoons melted butter

Makes 30–32 pancakes (4 inch diameter).

Method
Sift all-purpose flour, baking powder, salt and baking soda into a bowl and add the buckwheat flour and sugar (if used). Make a well in the center and add the buttermilk, melted butter and molasses, if used. Stir until mixed, then gradually draw in the flour mixture until the batter is almost smooth. Let stand 2 hours or more — the batter keeps well in the refrigerator for 2–3 days. Cook the pancakes as for regular pancakes (page 111) and serve with melted butter, maple syrup or honey, or with sour cream and fruit compote or homemade preserves.

Deep Fried Pancakes

2 eggs
½ cup flour
pinch of salt
¾ cup milk or half milk and half water, mixed
1 tablespoon melted butter
¼ cup butter (for frying)
2 cup quantity of orange pastry cream (for filling) – see box
deep fat (for frying)
orange slices (for garnish) – see box
confectioners' sugar (for sprinkling)

For coating
2 eggs, beaten to mix
¼ cup whole blanched almonds, finely chopped

Makes about 12 pancakes.

Method
Make the orange pastry cream for the filling, cover tightly and let cool.

To make the pancakes: beat the eggs in a bowl with a fork until mixed, then stir in the flour, salt and milk or milk and water mixture alternately, still using the fork. Add the melted butter and beat until the batter is smooth.

In a heavy frying pan or skillet, heat the butter and add 1–2 tablespoons batter, quickly tilting and turning the pan so the bottom is evenly coated. Cook over medium heat until the pancake is just set on top and golden brown on the bottom. Turn out onto a cloth and continue frying the remaining pancakes in the same way.

Put a spoonful of filling in the center of each pancake, brush the edges with beaten egg and wrap up like a parcel. Brush the pancakes all over with beaten egg and roll them in ground almonds until well coated. Chill until the coating is firm.

Heat the deep fat to 375°F on a fat thermometer and fry the pancakes, a few at a time, until they are golden brown.
Watchpoint: do not overcook them or they will burst.

Drain the pancakes on paper towels and keep them hot in a warm oven with the door open while frying the remaining pancakes.

Arrange the pancakes on a hot platter, sprinkle with confectioners' sugar, decorate with orange slices and serve at once.

Orange Pastry Cream

Beat 2 egg yolks with ½ cup sugar until the mixture is thick and light. Stir in 1½ tablespoons flour, pinch of salt and 1 tablespoon cornstarch with the grated rind of 2 oranges. Add 1 tablespoon cold milk to make a smooth paste.

Scald 1 cup light cream and gradually pour it into the egg mixture, stirring. Return the mixture to the pan and bring to a boil over low heat, stirring constantly. Cook 2 minutes, stirring, take from the heat and stir in ¼ cup Grand Marnier, Triple Sec, Curacao or other orange liqueur. Cover the pastry cream tightly and let cool.

Orange and Lemon Slices

A small cutter for removing even strips of peel from oranges and lemons is available in many specialty kitchen shops. Use it to remove strips of peel, at evenly spaced intervals, working from the top to the bottom of the fruit, then cut the fruit in slices — the peel will be decorated as shown in the photograph on the right.

Note: strips of peel have too much bitter pith attached to be used when the 'zest' (thinly pared rind of oranges and lemons) is called for in a recipe.

Deep fried pancakes are filled with orange pastry cream and decorated with orange slices

Children will be delighted by a selection of party treats that includes gingerbread men, sandwiches garnished like gaily colored flowers, and a cranberry punch.

Parents will have a chance to enjoy their own informal party with a buffet spread of hot and cold dishes and a potent cider punch to go with them.

PARTY TREATS FOR CHILDREN AND PARENTS

Children's Treats

Flower Sandwiches
Pineapple & Cheese Sticks
Gingerbread Men   Gingerbread House
Assorted Cookies

Cranberry Punch

Parents' Party

Bean & Tomato Soup
Beef Hot Pot
Pinwheel Salad
Garlic Loaf
Assorted Cookies

Cider Punch

CHILDREN'S TREATS

Quantities
The recipes on pages 116–119 make enough for 25–30 children.

TIMETABLE

Flower sandwiches: make in morning; keep covered with plastic wrap.

Butterscotch corn flake cookies: make in morning; keep covered with plastic wrap.

Gingerbread men: make the dough, shape, bake and decorate 2–3 days before; store in airtight container.

Gingerbread house: make the dough, shape, bake and decorate 2–3 days before; store in airtight container. Assemble day before serving.

Chocolate marshmallow squares: make and bake 2–3 days before; store in airtight container.

Peanut balls: make and bake 2–3 days before; store in airtight container.

Raisin oatmeal drops: make and bake 2–3 days before; store in airtight container.

Cranberry punch: combine the fruit juices in the morning and chill. Add remaining ingredients just before serving.

Flower Sandwiches

Make flower sandwiches from an unsliced loaf of firm-textured white or brown bread.

Cut the bread into about $\frac{1}{2}$ inch thick slices and cut out rounds with a 2–3 inch cookie cutter.

Spread the rounds with softened butter or cream cheese and arrange a 'flower' design on each one. For example, make a daisy by cutting petals from the white of a hard-cooked egg; the sieved yolk makes the golden center with a very thin strip of cucumber peel for the stem and leaves.

Cut flowerpots from a tomato, with crushed tuna for the blossoms and small watercress leaves for the greenery.

Shape marigolds with petals cut from thin slices of carrot, a parsley stalk for stem and tiny sprigs of parsley for leaves.

Pineapple and Cheese Sticks

Drain 1 medium (14 oz) can pineapple chunks or cut 1 medium fresh pineapple into squares. Cut 1 lb Cheddar cheese into squares. Spear a chunk of pineapple and cheese with a toothpick and arrange the sticks on a platter.

Basic Gingerbread Dough

4 cups flour
1 tablespoon baking soda
$\frac{1}{2}$ teaspoon salt
2 teaspoons ground ginger
$\frac{1}{2}$ teaspoon ground cinnamon
$\frac{1}{2}$ cup butter
1 cup dark brown sugar
1 cup molasses
$1\frac{1}{2}$–2 tablespoons milk

Method
Sift the flour with the baking soda, salt and spices into a bowl.

Heat the butter, sugar and molasses in a saucepan over low heat until the butter is melted and the sugar is dissolved. Let the mixture cool a little, then mix it with the flour mixture and enough milk to make a firm dough.

Wrap the dough in wax paper and chill 30 minutes before rolling it out and shaping.

Gingerbread Men

4 cup quantity of basic gingerbread dough

For decoration
raisins
candied cherries
1 cup royal icing (see page 71)

Pastry bag and writing tube; gingerbread man cutter (optional)

Makes about 24 men, 6 inches high.

Method
Set the oven at moderately low (325°F). Grease several baking sheets.

Roll out the dough to $\frac{1}{4}$ inch thickness. Cut out the men with the cutter, or shape a cardboard pattern and grease underneath the pattern before laying it on the dough and cutting around it with a small sharp knife.

When all gingerbread men are cut out, transfer them carefully with a small spatula to the baking sheets. Press in raisins for their eyes and vest buttons and a small piece of candied cherry for the mouth.

Bake in heated oven for 10–15 minutes or until gingerbread is lightly browned. Cool a little before removing them from the baking sheet.

Put the icing in the pastry bag fitted with the writing tube and outline the eyebrows, nose, tie, belt, cuffs and shoes.

Gingerbread House

4 cup quantity of basic gingerbread dough
1 cup royal icing (see page 71)

For sugar syrup
1 cup sugar
$\frac{1}{2}$ cup water

Pastry bag; medium writing tube and $\frac{1}{4}$ inch plain tube

Method
Set the oven at moderately low (325°F). Grease several baking sheets.

Cut out paper guides for the gingerbread dough: for long walls, 1 rectangle 10 X 5 inches; for the roof, 1 rectangle 10 X 4 inches; for short end walls, 1 piece, basically 5 inches square rising to a gable with 4 inch sides; for the chimney, a 2 inch square.

Roll out the gingerbread dough to about one-eighth

inch thickness. Use the paper guides to cut out 4 walls (2 long, and 2 short with gable), 2 roof pieces and 4 chimney pieces.

Place the sections on the baking sheets and bake in heated oven for 10–15 minutes or until the gingerbread springs back when lightly pressed with a finger-tip.

When the gingerbread pieces are cold, decorate them with royal icing. Using the pastry bag fitted with the writing tube, mark the windows, doors and the tiles on the roof.

To make the sugar syrup: heat the sugar with the water until dissolved, then boil to the 'medium crack' stage when a little syrup dropped in a cup of cold water forms a brittle ball (270°F on a sugar thermometer). Stand the base of the pan in hot water to stop the syrup from cooking but keep it liquid.

Join the pieces of gingerbread together by dipping the edges in sugar syrup.
Note: cut V-shaped pieces out of the base of the side-pieces of the chimney so the chimney fits on the roof. Cover the joins with a thick border of icing, using the pastry bag fitted with the $\frac{1}{4}$ inch plain tube.

(Above, right) Using paper guides, cut out of the ginger-bread dough the walls and other sections of the house.

(Right) Dip edges of the gingerbread pieces in the sugar syrup and join together to form the house

Chocolate Marshmallow Squares

$\frac{1}{2}$ cup shortening
$\frac{3}{4}$ cup flour
$\frac{1}{4}$ teaspoon baking powder
$\frac{1}{4}$ teaspoon salt
$\frac{3}{4}$ cup sugar
2 tablespoons dry cocoa
2 eggs
1 teaspoon vanilla
$\frac{1}{2}$ cup chopped pecans

For glaze
2 squares (2 oz) unsweetened chocolate, cut in pieces
2 squares (2 oz) semisweet chocolate, cut in pieces
$\frac{1}{4}$ cup butter
2 teaspoons honey
$\frac{1}{2}$ cup miniature marshmallows

9 inch square pan

Makes 18 squares.

Method
Set the oven at moderate (350°F); grease the pan.

In a large saucepan melt the shortening over a low heat. Remove pan from heat and stir in the flour, baking powder, salt, sugar, cocoa, eggs, vanilla and pecans; stir to mix well. Spread the mixture in the prepared pan and bake in heated oven for 25–30 minutes or until the cake pulls away from the sides of the pan. Cool.

To make the glaze: melt both kinds of chocolate, butter and honey in a pan over hot water until the chocolate melts and the glaze is smooth. Remove from heat, cool slightly and stir in the marshmallows.

Cut the cooled cake into 18 squares and spread glaze on each one. Refrigerate just until the glaze is set.

Party treats

Raisin oatmeal drops are piled in the bowl and chocolate marshmallow squares and peanut balls are arranged on the glass platter

Raisin Oatmeal Drops

1 cup raisins
1 cup quick-cooking rolled oats
2 cups flour
1 teaspoon baking soda
½ teaspoon salt
1 teaspoon ground cinnamon
1 teaspoon ground nutmeg
¾ cup shortening
1 cup brown sugar, firmly packed
2 eggs, beaten to mix
1 tablespoon grated orange rind
2 tablespoons orange juice
½ cup chopped walnuts

Makes 48–60 cookies.

Method

Set the oven at moderately hot (375°F). Grease 2 baking sheets.

Sift the flour with the baking soda, salt, cinnamon, and nutmeg into a bowl. Cream the shortening, gradually add the brown sugar and beat until soft and light. Beat in the eggs, grated orange rind and orange juice. Add the raisins, rolled oats, walnuts and flour mixture and stir until thoroughly mixed.

Drop heaping teaspoons of the mixture onto the greased baking sheets and flatten the surfaces with a fork. Bake in heated oven for 10–12 minutes or until the cookies are a light brown. Cool before serving.

Peanut Balls

⅔ cup peanut butter
½ cup chopped peanuts
1½ cups sugar
¾ cup flour
½ cup butter
½ cup milk
1½ cups quick-cooking rolled oats
½ cup sweetened, shredded coconut
1 teaspoon vanilla
¼ teaspoon salt
1 egg white (for brushing)
1 cup sweetened, shredded coconut or finely chopped peanuts (for rolling)

Makes about 60 cookies.

Method

Combine the sugar, flour, butter and milk in a large saucepan. Heat gently until melted, bring to a boil and cook 3 minutes, stirring constantly. Remove from heat and stir in all the remaining ingredients, except egg white and nuts for rolling.

Roll the dough into walnut-sized balls between the palms of your hands. Brush the balls with a little egg white, roll them in additional coconut or chopped peanuts and let dry at room temperature for 3–4 hours.

Butterscotch Corn Flake Cookies

4 cups corn flakes
¾ cup dark brown sugar
1 tablespoon honey
1½ tablespoons butter
½ cup milk

Makes about 20 cookies.

Method

Mix the sugar, honey, butter and milk together in a saucepan and cook over low heat until the mixture forms a soft ball when a little is dropped in cold water (240°F on a sugar thermometer).

Meanwhile toast corn flakes in a moderate oven (350°F) for 10 minutes or until brown. Put them in a lightly buttered mixing bowl. Pour in the hot syrup mixture and mix thoroughly with a fork.

Using 2 forks, shape the mounds as quickly as possible on a buttered baking sheet. Let stand until cold before removing the cookies from the sheet.

Cranberry Punch

4½ cups cranberry juice
3 cups orange juice
¾ cup lemon juice
1½ quarts ginger ale
1½ cups sugar syrup (made by heating 1 cup sugar with ½ cup water until the sugar is dissolved)
2 lemons, thinly sliced

Serves 18–20 people.

Method

Combine the cranberry, orange and lemon juices. Just before serving, add ice cubes to the punch, pour in the ginger ale and sweeten to taste with the sugar syrup. Float lemon slices on top.

PARENTS' PARTY

TIMETABLE

Bean and tomato soup: make 2–3 days before and refrigerate but do not add kneaded butter. Before serving, reheat and add kneaded butter, if using.

Beef hot pot: prepare 1–2 days before, cover and refrigerate; reheat in hot oven (400°F) 15–20 minutes until very hot.

Pinwheel salad: make dough 1 day ahead, cover and refrigerate before second rising. In the morning prepare salads, but do not add dressing; cover and refrigerate. Let dough rise again; bake. When cold, spread filling, finish salads and assemble pinwheel.

Garlic loaf: bake just before serving.

Cider punch: prepare in the morning. If serving hot, bake oranges and lemons. Heat punch before serving.

Quantities
The recipes on these pages serve 10 people.

Bean and Tomato Soup

1 cup (½ lb) dried kidney beans
1 tablespoon tomato paste
2 cups (1 lb) canned Italian-type
   plum tomatoes
1 lb stew beef
2 tablespoons oil
2 onions, chopped
1 teaspoon chili powder
2 teaspoons thyme or marjoram
2 quarts beef stock or water
salt and pepper
kneaded butter (made with
   2 tablespoons butter and
   1 tablespoon flour) – optional

Method
Soak beans overnight in water to cover and drain.

Cut the beef in small pieces and brown them quickly in the oil with the onions. Add the drained beans, tomato paste, tomatoes, chili powder, herbs and stock or water.

Season, bring to a boil, cover and simmer 2 hours or until the beans are very soft. If you like, thicken the soup by stirring in the kneaded butter, a piece at a time, and simmering it for 2 minutes.

Garlic Loaf

Cut a large loaf of French or Italian bread into 1½ inch slices, cutting through to within ½ inch of the bottom.

Crush 1–2 cloves of garlic with a pinch of salt in a bowl and work in ¼–½ cup butter (depending on size of loaf) until creamy. Spread this on both sides of each slice, reserving a little butter, and press the loaf back into shape.

Spread the top and sides with remaining butter, wrap in foil and bake in a hot oven (400°F) for 12–15 minutes, opening the foil for the last 5 minutes to make the bread crisp.

For less garlic flavor, cut one clove into quarters but do not crush it. Cream the butter, add the quartered clove and let stand for 30 minutes. Remove the garlic quarters, spread the butter on the bread and bake as above.

Beef Hot Pot

4 lb flank steak, cut into
   1½ inch cubes
2 tablespoons oil
4–5 onions, sliced
1–2 tablespoons flour
2½ cups ale
2 cups beef stock
.1 teaspoon sugar
1 teaspoon wine vinegar
salt
black pepper, freshly ground
2 cups (½ lb) mushrooms,
   halved
6 medium potatoes, peeled
   and sliced
2 teaspoons melted butter

Method
Set oven at moderate (350°F).

Heat the oil in a large shallow flameproof casserole and brown the meat on all sides, a few pieces at a time. Remove meat from the casserole, reduce the heat, add the onions and cook slowly until they are golden brown. Sprinkle in enough flour to absorb the remaining fat and cook, stirring frequently, until lightly browned.

Add the ale and stock and cook, stirring, until boiling. Add the sugar and wine vinegar, replace the meat and season with salt and pepper. Cover tightly and bake in heated oven for about 2 hours.

Add the mushrooms to the hot pot and lay potato slices on top of the meat. Baste them with the casserole juices and brush with melted butter. Return the pot, uncovered, to the oven; bake about 45 minutes longer or until the potatoes are crisp and brown.

Pinwheel Salad

For dough
2 cups flour
½ teaspoon salt
1 package dry or 1 cake
   compressed yeast
⅓ cup lukewarm milk
2 eggs, beaten to mix
1 teaspoon sugar
¼ cup butter, softened
¼ cup butter or cream cheese,
   flavored with a little Dijon-
   style mustard (for filling)

For topping
1 cooked beet, coarsely grated
2 tablespoons vinaigrette
   dressing
½ cucumber, thinly sliced
2 carrots, grated
1 onion, cut into thin rings and
   blanched
4–5 medium tomatoes, peeled
   and thinly sliced
1 cup cole slaw

Method
To make the dough: sift the flour and salt into a warm bowl. Sprinkle the yeast over the lukewarm milk and leave 5 minutes or until dissolved. Stir into the beaten eggs with the sugar.

Make a well in the center of the flour, add the liquid, stir until mixed and knead thoroughly until the dough is smooth and elastic. Work the softened butter into the mixture, cover the dough with a cloth and let rise in a warm place for 40 minutes or until almost doubled in bulk.

Set the oven at hot (400°F).

Pat out the dough on a floured baking sheet into a 12–14 inch circle. Let stand in a warm place for 15 minutes or until well risen, then bake in heated oven for about 25–30 minutes or until lightly browned.

When cold, split the circle of bread in half and spread one surface with mustard-flavored butter or cream cheese. Cover with the other half and arrange the salads on top as follows.

In the center put a mound of grated beets mixed with a little vinaigrette dressing. Surround this with thin slices of cucumber, then grated carrot. Arrange overlapping slices of tomato around the carrot and place an onion ring between each tomato slice. Arrange the cole slaw around the edge so the whole surface of the bread is covered.

For dessert, share the children's cookies and serve them with coffee.

Cider Punch

A well-made punch is a refreshing change for guests. In the fall, one of the great treats is fresh apple cider and this specialty of the season can also be the basis for a simple but delicious punch. If fresh cider is not available, regular cider can be used.

To 2 parts cider add 1 part apple brandy. To give the punch a little color, as well as to heighten the apple flavor, add the rind or slices of several oranges and lemons.

Pour the mixture over a block of ice in a large punch bowl or, to make a less diluted drink, keep it in a pitcher and pour it into individual glasses 'on the rocks'.

On a cold day, you may want to try a hot version of the same punch. The liquid ingredients are the same, but a pinch of spice – like cinnamon or nutmeg – improves it. In a moderate oven (350°F), bake 3–4 quartered oranges and lemons, stuck with cloves, for 30 minutes or until golden brown. Heat 1 part cider and 1 part brandy with spice over medium heat until hot but not boiling, transfer to a punch bowl and add the fruit.

Top a mustard-flavored butter or cheese-filled bread with a selection of vegetables for a colorful pinwheel salad

To accompany a trio of puddings (from left to right): serve baked sponge pudding with red jam sauce, Eve's pudding with orange cream sauce, and individual Valencia puddings with banana sauce

HOW TO MAKE SAUCES (2) SWEET

Unlike most savory sauces, sweet sauces are not based on a standard recipe. They can be divided into different categories — chocolate sauces, fruit and hard sauces, and those using eggs, such as the hot and cold sabayon, and sweet mousseline.

Some of these sauces have appeared in previous Volumes but they are repeated here for convenience.

FRUIT SAUCES

Fruit and jam sauces are usually served with ice cream, molded desserts, baked or steamed puddings and simple, unfrosted cakes. Some of them, however, are ideal accompaniments to roasts of rich meats and cold meats.

Note: the quantities given in these sauce recipes make 1–1½ cups.

Banana Sauce

1 banana, thinly sliced
juice of ½ lemon, with enough water to make 1 cup liquid
1 tablespoon Maraschino liqueur or juice from Maraschino cherries
2 tablespoons sugar
2 teaspoons arrowroot (mixed to a paste with 1 tablespoon water)

Serve with vanilla ice cream or baked sponge puddings.

Method
Put the lemon juice, water and Maraschino liqueur or cherry juice into a pan with the sugar and dissolve over gentle heat. Stir in the arrowroot paste and cook, stirring, until the sauce thickens and is clear.

Add the sliced banana and serve hot.

Orange Cream Sauce

1 large or 2 small oranges
5 cubes of sugar
¾ cup heavy cream, whipped until it holds a soft shape

For custard
¾ cup milk
2 egg yolks
1 teaspoon sugar
1 teaspoon arrowroot

This sauce is good with fruit fritters and apple dumplings.

Method
To make the custard: scald the milk. Beat the egg yolks with the sugar and arrowroot until smooth, pour on the milk, return the mixture to the pan and cook over low heat, stirring, until the custard thickens.
Watchpoint: do not let it boil.

With a vegetable peeler, thinly peel the rind from half the orange, cut it into fine strips and cook it in boiling water for 5 minutes or until tender. Drain well.

Rub the sugar cubes over the remaining orange peel to remove all the zest (oil) – each cube should be completely saturated with oil. Strain the juice from the orange, add 5 tablespoons to the sugar cubes and stir until the sugar is dissolved.

Stir the orange syrup into the whipped cream, together with the cold custard and strips of orange rind. Serve cold.

Apricot Jam, Red Jam or Marmalade Sauce

¼ cup thick apricot jam, any red jam or marmalade
1 cup water
2 strips of lemon rind (if using apricot jam or marmalade)
1 tablespoon sugar
1–2 teaspoons arrowroot (mixed to a paste with 1–2 tablespoons water) – optional

Serve with crêpes or baked sponge desserts.

Method
Put all the ingredients except the arrowroot paste in a pan and bring slowly to a boil, stirring. Taste and, if the flavor is bland, add more jam. Simmer 5–6 minutes and strain.

If the sauce is thin, add a little arrowroot paste and simmer until thickened.

Apricot Jam Sauce with Rum

½ cup apricot jam
2 tablespoons rum
½ cup water
juice of 1 lemon

Method
Put the jam, water and lemon juice in a pan and heat gently until the jam is melted. Bring to a boil, take from heat and add the rum.

Strain the sauce into a bowl and serve cold.

Melba sauce

1 pint fresh raspberries or 1 package frozen raspberries (thawed)
2 tablespoons confectioners' sugar (or to taste)

Serve cold over vanilla ice cream topped with poached peaches or pears, or with a dessert like almond meringue cake (see Volume 4) and hazelnut meringue cake (see page 91).

Method
Pick over fresh raspberries. Work the fresh or frozen raspberries through a nylon strainer or purée in a blender and strain to remove the seeds. Beat in the sugar a tablespoon at a time.

Pineapple Sauce

¾ cup finely chopped fresh pineapple or 1 can (8½ oz) crushed pineapple
2 tablespoons sugar (or to taste)
2 teaspoons cornstarch
pinch of salt
¾ cup unsweetened pineapple juice
1 teaspoon lemon juice

Method
Mix the sugar with the cornstarch and salt, stir in the pineapple juice and bring to a boil, stirring. Simmer 2 minutes, take from heat, stir in the lemon juice and pineapple. Serve hot or cold.

Walnut and Apple Sauce

$\frac{1}{4}$ cup coarsely chopped
    walnuts
3 tart apples, cored, quartered
    and sliced
1 tablespoon butter
peeled rind of $\frac{1}{2}$ lemon
6 tablespoons sugar
$\frac{1}{2}$ cup water

Serve this sauce with ice cream, caramel and vanilla bavarois or rice pudding.

Method

Spread the butter in a skillet, add the apples and then the lemon rind. Cover with foil, put on the lid, and cook over gentle heat until the apples are pulpy. Remove the lemon rind and work the mixture through a strainer or purée in a blender.

Dissolve the sugar in water over low heat, bring to a boil and simmer 3–4 minutes or until the syrup thickens slightly.

Take from the heat, stir in the apple purée and simmer, stirring, until the mixture is thick but still pours easily. Add the walnuts and cook 1 minute longer. Serve hot or cold.

Red Wine Sauce

2 tablespoons red wine
1 tablespoon sugar
$\frac{3}{4}$ cup water
2 tablespoons raspberry, red
    currant or blackberry jelly
    or jam
2 strips of lemon rind
1 teaspoon arrowroot (mixed
    to a paste with 1 tablespoon
    water)

Serve with hot vanilla soufflé or poached pears.

Method

Put the sugar, water, jelly or jam and lemon rind in a pan and bring slowly to a boil. Simmer about 8 minutes. Stir in the arrowroot paste and cook until the sauce is thickened and clear. Take from the heat, add the wine, strain and serve hot.

Cumberland Sauce

2–3 strips of orange rind and
    juice of 1 orange
$\frac{1}{2}$ cup red currant jelly
juice of $\frac{1}{2}$ lemon
$\frac{1}{4}$ cup port

Serve with cold meats.

Method

Cut the rind into thin strips and blanch in boiling water for 1 minute. Drain, refresh and drain them again.

Over gentle heat melt the red currant jelly with the lemon juice, port and the juice from the orange. Let cool before adding the orange rind.

Plain Cherry Sauce

1 lb tart or dark sweet red
    cherries
2–3 tablespoons sugar
pinch of ground cinnamon
about $\frac{1}{2}$ cup water
squeeze of lemon juice
    (optional)
2 teaspoons arrowroot (mixed
    to a paste with 1 tablespoon
    water)

This cherry sauce is good with any type of angel food or sponge cake.

Method

Pit the cherries and combine in a pan with the sugar and cinnamon. Cover and set on a low heat until the juice runs freely. Remove cherries with a slotted spoon. Add the water to the juice, simmer 5 minutes and take from heat. Taste for sweetness, adding more sugar if you like; if too sweet, add a little lemon juice.

Stir the arrowroot paste into the cherry syrup. Bring just to a boil, stirring, and take from the heat — the liquid should be the consistency of heavy cream. Add the cherries to the pan. If the sauce is to be served hot, reheat.

Orange and Red Currant Sauce

rind and juice of 1 orange
$\frac{1}{4}$ cup red currant jelly
1 tablespoon chopped mint
1 tablespoon white wine
    vinegar

Serve with roast meat.

Method

In a bowl mix the rind and juice of the orange (when grating orange, take care to remove only the outer rind and none of the white pith); add the red currant jelly and stir until it is well mixed. If the jelly is very firm, warm it carefully in a saucepan before adding to the orange rind and juice.

Stir in the chopped mint and white wine vinegar and serve the sauce in a small bowl.

CHOCOLATE SAUCES

Rich chocolate sauce and Suchard sauce are good with puddings and baked desserts, sweet choux (cream puffs) and ice cream. For an especially rich dessert of ice cream or profiteroles, choose fudge sauce.

Chocolate Sauce

2 squares (2 oz) unsweetened chocolate, cut in pieces
½ cup sugar
¾ cup water
1 teaspoon vanilla

Method
In a pan dissolve the sugar in the water over gentle heat, then bring to a boil and boil 5 minutes.

Add the pieces of chocolate and cook, stirring, until the chocolate is melted. Take from the heat and stir in the vanilla.

Note: the quantities given in these sauce recipes make 1–1½ cups.

Suchard Sauce

6 squares (6 oz) unsweetened chocolate, grated
2 cups water
½ cup sugar
pinch of salt
½ teaspoon vanilla

Method
Melt the chocolate with the water in a pan over low heat, stirring occasionally. When smooth, add the sugar and salt and stir until dissolved. Bring the sauce to a boil and simmer, uncovered, until it is rich and syrupy. Take from the heat and add the vanilla.

Serve hot or cold – if serving hot, simmer the sauce until it is slightly thicker than if serving cold.

Rich Chocolate Sauce

2 squares (2 oz) semisweet chocolate
2 tablespoons sugar
1 teaspoon cocoa
1 teaspoon dry instant coffee
1½ cups water
1 egg yolk (optional)
1 teaspoon vanilla

Method
Cut up the chocolate and put it in a saucepan with the sugar, cocoa, coffee and water. Heat slowly, stirring frequently until dissolved, then simmer, uncovered for 20 minutes or until the sauce is the consistency of heavy cream.

Take from the heat and, if using an egg yolk, stir 1–2 tablespoons of the hot sauce into the egg yolk and stir into the remaining mixture in the pan. Add the vanilla.

If not using an egg yolk, simmer the sauce until it is a little thicker before adding the vanilla. Serve hot or cold.

Orange Chocolate Sauce

1 orange
6 squares (6oz) unsweetened chocolate, cut in pieces
4 cubes of sugar
1½ cups water
½ cup granulated sugar
pinch of salt

Method
Rub the sugar cubes over the orange until they are saturated with zest (oil).

Melt the pieces of chocolate in the water over gentle heat, add the sugar and salt and simmer, uncovered, until the sauce is syrupy and coats the back of a spoon.

Take sauce from the heat, stir in the orange-soaked sugar cubes until dissolved. Chill.

Fudge Sauce

1 package (12 oz) semisweet chocolate pieces
2 squares (2 oz) unsweetened chocolate, grated
pinch of salt
3 tablespoons strong coffee
1 cup heavy cream
2 tablespoons brandy (optional)

Serve as a hot fudge sauce with chocolate, vanilla or coffee ice cream or steamed chocolate puddings.

Method
Put both kinds of chocolate, salt and the coffee in the top of a double boiler. Let the chocolate melt over hot water, then gradually stir in the cream and brandy if used. Stir until smooth. Serve hot or cool.

HARD SAUCES

All hard sauces are variations of a basic mixture of equal quantities of unsalted butter and granulated, brown or confectioners' sugar, beaten until soft and light, with an added flavoring. They are served with the traditional Christmas plum pudding, with other steamed puddings such as fig or date, with apple pie and gingerbread.

Rum Hard Sauce

2–3 tablespoons rum (or to taste)
6 tablespoons unsalted butter
6 tablespoons dark brown sugar
grated rind of ½ lemon and a squeeze of lemon juice

Method
Cream the butter and gradually beat in the sugar with the lemon rind and juice. When soft and light, beat in enough rum, a little at a time, to flavor the butter well. Pile in a small bowl and chill before serving.

Brandy Hard Sauce

Make in the same way as rum butter using 6 tablespoons unsalted butter, 6 tablespoons sugar and 2–3 tablespoons brandy (or to taste).

Lemon Hard Sauce

juice of $\frac{1}{2}$ lemon
grated rind of 1 lemon
6 tablespoons unsalted butter
6 tablespoons granulated or
confectioners' sugar

Serve with crêpes.

Method
Cream the butter with the lemon rind and gradually beat in the sugar with lemon juice. Beat the mixture until light and fluffy. Pile in a small bowl and chill until firm.

Spicy Hard Sauce

5 tablespoons butter
1 cup confectioners' sugar
large pinch of salt
1 teaspoon vanilla
$\frac{1}{2}$ teaspoon ground cinnamon
$\frac{1}{2}$ teaspoon lemon juice
$\frac{1}{4}$ teaspoon ground cloves

Method
Cream the butter until it is soft. Sift the confectioners' sugar and add it gradually to the butter. Beat well until blended, add the salt, vanilla, cinnamon, lemon juice and cloves. Beat until blended; chill.

EGG SAUCES

The following three sauces are made with eggs beaten with sugar and flavoring until light and frothy.

Hot Sabayon Sauce 1

3 egg yolks
1 tablespoon sugar
$\frac{1}{2}$ cup sherry
small strip of lemon rind

Serve with fruit desserts.

Method
Combine all the ingredients in the top of a double boiler and whisk over hot but not boiling water until the mixture is very frothy and slightly thick. Remove the lemon rind and serve.

Hot Sabayon Sauce 2

2 eggs
2 egg yolks
6 tablespoons sugar
$\frac{1}{4}$ cup sherry or fruit juice

Serve with sponge puddings.

Method
Put all the ingredients in the top of a double boiler and whisk over hot but not boiling water until the sauce is thick and frothy. Do not overcook or it will separate. Serve warm.

Watchpoint: use this sauce as soon as possible; if it must be kept for a short time, whisk it again for 1 minute before serving.

Cold Sabayon Sauce

$\frac{1}{4}$ cup sugar
$\frac{1}{4}$ cup water
2 egg yolks
grated rind and juice of
$\frac{1}{2}$ lemon
1 tablespoon rum or brandy
or 2 tablespoons sherry
$\frac{3}{4}$ cup heavy cream, whipped
until it holds a soft shape

Serve with fresh fruit, and fruit desserts.

Method
Dissolve the sugar in the water over gentle heat, then boil the syrup until it spins a thread between your finger and thumb when a little is lifted out on a spoon (230°F–234°F on a sugar thermometer).

Beat the egg yolks well, take the syrup from the heat and, as soon as the bubbles have subsided, pour it gradually into the egg yolks, beating constantly. Continue beating until the mixture is very thick.

Beat in the lemon rind and juice. Flavor with rum, brandy or sherry and beat 1–2 minutes longer or until cool. Fold the whipped cream into the mixture and chill.

Crème à la Vanille (Vanilla Custard Sauce)

1½ cups milk
2 tablespoons sugar
½ teaspoon vanilla extract or
    ½ vanilla bean, split
3 egg yolks

Method

Put milk in a pan with sugar and heat until dissolved; if using vanilla bean, infuse it in the milk for 10 minutes, keeping pan covered. Take out bean, then add the sugar.

Beat egg yolks in a bowl until lightly colored, scald the vanilla-flavored milk and gradually stir into yolks. Return to pan and stir with a wooden spoon over gentle heat. When custard coats the back of a spoon and looks creamy, strain back into the bowl. Add the vanilla if using. Sprinkle with a little sugar and cool. This coating of sugar melts and helps to prevent a skin from forming.
Watchpoint: if the custard gets too hot and starts to curdle, pour it at once into the bowl without straining and whisk briskly for 10 seconds.

Strawberry Custard Sauce

Serve with ice cream or fruit.

To 1½ cups crème à la vanille add 1 tablespoon kirsch or lemon juice and strawberry purée made from ½ cup fresh or frozen strawberries worked through a sieve or puréed in a blender.

MORE SWEET SAUCES

Caramel Sauce

¾ cup sugar
5 tablespoons cold water
¾ cup warm water

This sauce can be served plain or with a sliced banana and a squeeze of lemon juice added just before serving. It is good with bavarois à la crème or with small sweet choux (cream puffs).

Method

In a pan dissolve the sugar in cold water over low heat, then boil rapidly until it is a dark brown caramel color. Take at once from the heat, carefully add the warm water and stir over the heat until the sugar is dissolved.

Boil the sauce rapidly until it is syrupy and cool it. If it is too thick when cold, add 1–2 tablespoons more warm water. Serve hot or cold.

Caramel Cream Sauce

6 tablespoons light brown sugar
1 tablespoon light corn syrup
1½ cups light cream
¼ cup butter
½ vanilla bean, split or
    ½ teaspoon vanilla extract
2 teaspoons arrowroot (mixed to a paste with 2 tablespoons water)

Serve hot with coffee parfait or vanilla or coffee ice cream.

Method

Put the sugar and corn syrup in a heavy pan and dissolve over gentle heat. In another pan heat the cream with the butter and vanilla bean, if using, cover and leave to infuse for about 10 minutes. Remove the vanilla bean.

Boil the sugar mixture until it begins to caramelize, then cook to a deep brown. At once take from the heat and carefully add the cream mixture. Stir until the caramel dissolves, heating if necessary, then beat until smooth.

Stir in the arrowroot paste and heat until the sauce is thickened. Take from the heat, add the vanilla extract, if using, and serve at once.

Butterscotch Sauce

⅓ cup butter
1 cup dark brown sugar, firmly packed
2 tablespoons light corn syrup
⅓ cup heavy cream

Serve with ice cream or cakes.

Method

Melt the butter over low heat. Stir in the brown sugar, syrup and heavy cream. Bring just to a boil, take from the heat and cool slightly before serving.

Rum Sauce

2–3 tablespoons dark rum (or to taste)
½ cup sugar
½ cup water
1 teaspoon fresh lime juice

Serve with rich fruit desserts.

Method

In a pan dissolve the sugar in the water over low heat, bring to a boil and boil for 5 minutes. Take from the heat and add the rum and lime juice. Serve hot or cold.

Note: the quantities given in these sauce recipes make 1–1½ cups.

Coffee ice cream is topped with rich hot butterscotch sauce

ROTISSERIE AND SLOW OVEN ROASTING

A delicious way to roast is with a rotisserie. The meat is basted constantly by its own juices as it revolves so the fat becomes crisp while the lean remains juicy. Perhaps the greatest pleasure is the sight and smell of the meat as it revolves and cooks to a succulent golden brown.

Traditional spit roasting over an open fire tends to be impractical, but many modern ovens have fittings for a rotisserie and special appliances are also available.

When rotisserie roasting is impossible, many experts today contend that the nearest equivalent is to roast at a lower temperature than with more conventional methods using moderate or high heat. Slow roasting has the advantages that the meat is more evenly cooked, needs less attention and there is less splattering of fat.

ROTISSERIE ROASTING

Points to remember

1 The meat should be at room temperature, so take it from the refrigerator 1–2 hours before cooking.

2 Rub the surface of the meat with freshly ground black pepper and other herbs and spices you like. If salt is rubbed into the cut surface of uncooked meat, it tends to draw out the juices so add it during cooking, not before.

Dry mustard or Worcestershire sauce is good with beef, and aromatic herbs like rosemary, thyme and basil go well with lamb and veal. Many people like to stud a roast of lamb with slivers of garlic.

A leg of lamb can be rotisserie roasted with the bone in, but a shoulder of lamb must be fully or partly boned.

Spices like mustard, ginger, allspice and cloves complement the richness of pork. A whole fresh ham is too large to rotisserie roast on most appliances and a half ham is best boned and stuffed – do not add too much as the stuffing will swell. Loin of pork and boned cuts from the shoulder are also good for rotisserie roasting.

3 Cuts with plenty of natural fat baste themselves during cooking, but veal, white-fleshed poultry like chicken and lean cuts of meat should be spread with butter, or barded by tying around a thin layer of pork fat before putting on the spit.

Ham can be basted with honey or a little brown sugar dissolved in orange juice to glaze during cooking.

4 When arranging meat on the rotisserie, be sure it is balanced so that it can turn evenly. As far as possible, cut surfaces should be exposed to the heat in order to seal them and retain the juices.

The rotisserie spit must not touch the bone as this upsets the distribution of heat and may stop it altogether.

5 Temperature and methods of cooking will vary with the type of appliance you use, so follow the advice given in manufacturer's instruction book.

In general, turn the heat very high at first until the meat just begins to brown, then reduce it. Baste the meat occasionally with the drippings.

Note: approximate cooking times can be estimated as shown in the charts below and on opposite page, but these may vary with the size and shape of the cut of meat and the amount of fat. The only accurate test is to use a meat thermometer and insert it into the thickest part of the lean meat; it must never touch the bone or rest on fat.

Gravy for rotisserie roasts can cause a problem if the drip tray cannot be placed over direct heat. If this is so, discard the fat from the tray and pour the meat juices that remain into a saucepan, scraping any congealed pieces from the drip tray. Add a cup of stock, season and simmer the gravy until the flavor is concentrated. If you like, thicken it with a little kneaded butter, or arrowroot mixed to a paste with water.

If the drip tray can be placed over direct heat, make gravy in the usual way, but be sure to discard as much fat as possible.

SLOW OVEN ROASTING

Points to remember

1 Prepare the meat as for rotisserie roasting, adding freshly ground black pepper with other seasonings you like.

2 Set the meat on a rack in a roasting pan. Cuts with bone should be set fat side up; it is not necessary to add extra fat or to baste them.

Boned and rolled cuts or those taken from boneless meat should be spread with a little meat drippings or butter; there is no need to baste, but turn the meat over halfway through cooking.

3 Fresh pork should be slow roasted in a moderate oven (350°F) and all other meats in a moderately low (325°F) oven.

ROTISSERIE ROASTING

MEAT	APPROXIMATE COOKING TIME	TEMPERATURE ON MEAT THERMOMETER
Beef (without bone)	12–18 minutes per lb	140°F (rare)
	18–25 minutes per lb	160°F (medium)
	25–30 minutes per lb	170°F (well done)
(with bone)	18–20 minutes per lb	140°F (rare)
	20–25 minutes per lb	160°F (medium)
	25–30 minutes per lb	170°F (well done)
Veal	25–35 minutes per lb	170°F
Pork	30–35 minutes per lb	170°F
Lamb	25–30 minutes per lb	160°F (rare)
	30–35 minutes per lb	175°F (well done)
Poultry (stuffed)	25–30 minutes per lb	190°F
(unstuffed)	20–25 minutes per lb	190°F

SLOW ROASTING

Set oven at moderate (350°F) for fresh pork and moderately low (325°F) for all other meats.

CUTS OF MEAT	APPROXIMATE ROASTING TIME	TEMPERATURE ON MEAT THERMOMETER
FRESH PORK		
loin	25–30 minutes per lb	170°F
picnic shoulder	30 minutes per lb	170°F
rolled	35 minutes per lb	170°F
cushion	35 minutes per lb	170°F
Boston butt	35–40 minutes per lb	170°F
leg: whole with bone	25 minutes per lb	170°F
boned whole	35 minutes per lb	170°F
half, with bone	40 minutes per lb	170°F
ham, whole (processed)	10–15 minutes per lb	160°F
shank, or butt, half	15 minutes per lb	160°F
LAMB		
leg	25 minutes per lb	160°F (rare)
	35 minutes per lb	175°F (well done)
shoulder: whole with bone	25 minutes per lb	160°F (rare)
	35 minutes per lb	175°F (well done)
rolled	35 minutes per lb	160°F (rare)
	45 minutes per lb	175°F (well done)
cushion	25 minutes per lb	160°F (rare)
	35 minutes per lb	175°F (well done)
rib	25 minutes per lb	160°F (rare)
	35 minutes per lb	175°F (well done)

CUTS OF MEAT	APPROXIMATE ROASTING TIME	TEMPERATURE ON MEAT THERMOMETER
BEEF		
standing rib	25 minutes per lb	140°F (rare)
	30 minutes per lb	160°F (medium)
	35 minutes per lb	170°F (well done)
rolled rib	30 minutes per lb	140°F (rare)
	35 minutes per lb	160°F (medium)
	45 minutes per lb	170°F (well done)
Delmonico (rib eye)	18 minutes per lb	140°F (rare)
	20 minutes per lb	160°F (medium)
	22 minutes per lb	170°F (well done
fillet (tenderloin), whole	45–60 minutes total	140°F (rare)
fillet (tenderloin), half	45–50 minutes total	140°F (rare)
rolled rump	30 minutes per lb	160°F (medium)
	35 minutes per lb	170°F (well done)
sirloin tip	40 minutes per lb	160°F (medium)
	45 minutes per lb	170°F (well done)
VEAL		
leg	30 minutes per lb	175°F
loin	30 minutes per lb	175°F
rib (rack)	35 minutes per lb	175°F
rolled shoulder	40 minutes per lb	175°F

MEASURING & MEASUREMENTS

The recipe quantities in the Course are measured in standard level teaspoons, tablespoons and cups and their equivalents are shown below. Any liquid pints and quarts also refer to U.S. standard measures.

When measuring dry ingredients, fill the cup or spoon to overflowing without packing down and level the top with a knife. All the dry ingredients, including flour, should be measured before sifting, although sifting may be called for later in the instructions.

Butter and margarine usually come in measured sticks (1 stick equals $\frac{1}{2}$ cup) and other bulk fats can be measured by displacement. For $\frac{1}{3}$ cup fat, fill the measuring cup $\frac{2}{3}$ full of water. Add fat until the water reaches the 1 cup mark. Drain the cup of water and the fat remaining equals $\frac{1}{3}$ cup.

For liquids, fill the measure to the brim, or to the calibration line.

Often quantities of seasonings cannot be stated exactly, for ingredients vary in the amount they require. The instructions 'add to taste' are literal, for it is impossible to achieve just the right balance of flavors in many dishes without tasting them.

Liquid measure	Volume equivalent
3 teaspoons	1 tablespoon
2 tablespoons	1 fluid oz
4 tablespoons	$\frac{1}{4}$ cup
16 tablespoons	1 cup or 8 fluid oz
2 cups	1 pint
2 pints	1 quart
4 quarts	1 gallon

OVEN TEMPERATURES

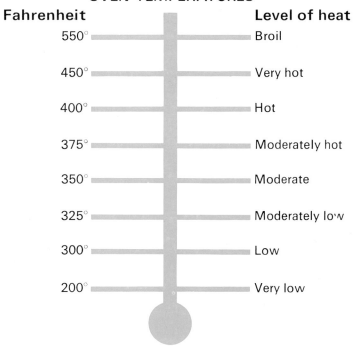

Fahrenheit	Level of heat
550°	Broil
450°	Very hot
400°	Hot
375°	Moderately hot
350°	Moderate
325°	Moderately low
300°	Low
200°	Very low

OVEN TEMPERATURES AND SHELF POSITIONS

Throughout the Cooking Course, oven temperatures are stated in degrees Fahrenheit and in generally agreed levels of heat such as 'high' and 'moderate'. The equivalents are shown on the table above.

However, exact temperature varies in different parts of an oven and the thermostat reading refers to the heat in the middle. As the oven temperature at top and bottom can vary as much as 25°F from this setting, the positioning of shelves is very important. In general, heat rises, so the hottest part of the oven is at the top, but consult the manufacturer's handbook about your individual model.

Pans and dishes of food should be placed parallel with burners or elements to avoid scorched edges.

When baking cakes, there must be room for the heat to circulate in the oven around baking sheets and cake pans; otherwise the underside of the cakes will burn. If baking more than one cake in an oven that has back burners or elements, arrange the cakes side by side. If the oven has side burners, arrange cakes back and front.

Oven thermostats are often inaccurate and are unreliable at extremely high or low temperatures. If you do a great deal of baking or question the accuracy of your oven, use a separate oven thermometer as a check on the thermostat.

Mid 18th-century scene in a London tea garden

Cooking Curiosities

Legend has it that the drinking of tea started around 2737 BC when a Chinese Emperor was waiting for a pot of water to boil and a few leaves fell into it, imparting a delicious aroma.

It wasn't until the middle of the 17th century that tea was introduced to the English by the Dutch, who bought it from Chinese trading boats off the island of Java.

Great Britain did not take to tea at once — it was considered a vicious beverage and used only as a cure for sickness. But by Queen Victoria's reign 'tea time' had become an institution.

Tea played an important role in the beginning of the United States. A monopoly given to the East India Company led in 1773 to the famous Boston Tea Party, when a group of Boston citizens threw the cargo from British tea ships into the sea rather than unload it and pay the tax. In retaliation, the British closed the port of Boston to all trade, thus sparking the Revolutionary War.

Now, as 200 years ago, most tea comes from Southeast Asia. There are three kinds: black or fermented; green or unfermented; and oolong or semi-fermented. The fermentation is the length of time the leaves are left on the bushes. Black teas, such as Pekoe, Pekoe Souchong, and Orange Pekoe, are the most widely used.

Green teas are made in China and Japan. These leaves, pulled from the bushes before they can wither, make a strongly scented tea that is very light and slightly green in color.

Oolong teas are made in Formosa and at one time were produced almost solely for export to the U.S., though now they are widely known.

Tea bags hold just enough tea to make one cup, but connoisseurs claim they can distinguish between tea made with leaves and a tea bag.

To make tea like the British, rinse out a china tea pot with boiling water, then add one teaspoon of leaves per person and one for the pot. Fill the tea pot with boiling water, put on the lid at once, then leave the tea to sit (steep) for 5 minutes. If it is too strong, dilute the tea with boiling water in the cup. Do not use less tea to make it weaker because some of the flavor will be lost. Green tea can stand for hours but black tea becomes bitter after 15 minutes.

The English drink tea (invariably black tea) with milk and sugar. However, the standard accompaniment to green tea is a slice of lemon or lime. The Chinese drink tea very weak and lukewarm; the Japanese have an elaborate ceremony; the Russians boil their water in a samovar and take their tea with lemon, and in Tibet they add a large piece of rancid yak butter.

INDEX

(Volume 9)

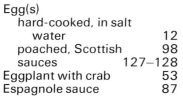

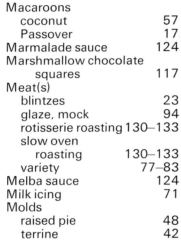

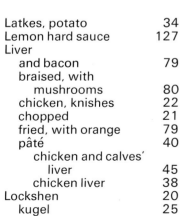

Acknowledgments
Photographs by Fred J. Maroon on pages 10, 13, 15, 16, 28 and 118. Photograph on page 56 by Pictor. Other photographs by Michael Leale, John Ledger, Roger Phillips, Michael Davies, Gina Harris and John Cowderoy.

NOTES